MARQUETRY & INLAY HANDBOOK

In Memory
of
Bessie Mae
Korzilius

MARQUETRY & INLAY HANDBOOK

Zachary Taylor

STERLING PUBLISHING CO., INC.
NEW YORK

This book is dedicated to Grahame Chambers and Manny Cefai,
my good friends and companion craftsmen of many years and many publications,
in acknowledgment of their respective skills in art and photography.
Z.T.

Library of Congress Cataloging-in-Publication Data
Taylor, Zachary.
  Marquetry & inlay handbook/Zachary Taylor.
      p. cm.
   ISBN 0-8069-2687-2
   1.   Marquetry. I. Title
TT192 T39 2002
745. 51'2-dc21

                              2002012601

                2 4 6 8 10 9 7 5 3 1

Published by Sterling Publishing Co., Inc.
387 Park Avenue South, New York, NY 10016
© 2003 by Zachary Taylor
Distributed in Canada by Sterling Publishing
^{c}/o Canadian Manda Group, One Atlantic Avenue, Suite 105
Toronto, Ontario, Canada M6K 3E7
Distributed in Great Britain by Chrysalis Books
64 Brewery Road, London N7 9NT, England
Distributed in Australia by Capricorn Link (Australia) Pty. Ltd.
P.O. Box 704, Windsor, NSW 2756, Australia

Printed in China
All rights reserved
Sterling ISBN 0-8069-2687-2

CONTENTS

ACKNOWLEDGMENTS

The author thanks the following, who helped in the production of this book:

Martin Brown, of BriMarc, for auxiliary equipment;

Cathy Challinor, Jane Julier, William Adams, Giovanni Aversa, Andrew Crawford and Arthur Lord, for permission to publish photographs of their work;

Nick Davidson, of Craft Supplies, for various woods;

Jennie Haines, for the supply of Dremel power tools;

Carl Holtey, for planes and channel cutters;

Leonard Lee, of Veritas Woodworking Tools, for special bench tools;

Stewart MacDonald, for luthiers' tools;

Chairperson Gretta Sherman and her fellow members of the Harrow Marquetry Society, for permitting the photographing and publication of their work;

Mike White, of Art Veneers, for the supply of all the veneers used throughout this book, for knives and auxiliary equipment;

Douglas Woodward, for the inclusion of Diamond Saws.

I–1. *This marquetry piece, the design of which is based on a famous painting by Vincent Van Gogh, was created using the scroll saw stack-cutting method described in Chapter 5.*

INTRODUCTION

Dear Reader,

There must be a good reason why you are reading this book, apart from its handsome cover and intriguing title. It could be that decorated wood has become especially captivating to you and thus you seek more information about the subject. Perhaps you have been attracted by an inlaid motif brightening an otherwise plain item of furniture. Or perhaps you have come across a fine old violin with elegant purfling* distinguishing its periphery? Maybe a handsome old writing slope has intrigued you with its banded corners in ebony and sycamore bordering an applied marquetry top?

Marquetry can be pictures created with a high artistic quality and inlays can enhance the most simple or sophisticated objects **(I-1)**; in the following pages, there are examples of excellence in all categories to inspire the enthusiast, beginner or experienced.

This book is concerned with the techniques of both marquetry and inlay, and it details the various ways of achieving, in each subject, high-quality results from simple methods. Tools that are used in this attractive craft need not be sophisticated, although some refined equipment is detailed, where appropriate, together with simple alternatives. Whether modern equipment or traditional hand tools are preferred, the application of each is detailed using basic examples to illustrate the methods. It is not necessary to have had any formal training in woodwork, or in any other craft, to embark on this fascinating subject.

* Purfling is the ornamental border on the backs and soundboards of stringed instruments.

I–2. *An inlayed and carved rose decorates the soundboard on this lute. The rosewood and tulipwood panel in the fingerboard is also inlayed.*

In the author's opinion, an onlooker should, on first contact with the marquetry or inlaid item, be appreciative of the artistic statement, rather than impressed with the skills involved or the woods selected. All too often, technique becomes the major area of concern in craft topics, with insufficient regard for aesthetics. While there is an abundance of common examples of applied technique with no vestige of art, there can be little doubt that few artistic statements can be made without

excellent technique. For instance, cartoon characters in vibrant primary colors have their place, but the potential for expressing subtlety and delicacy are special qualities available to the artist in wood.

Marquetry and inlaying are techniques that use fine woods to make pictures or to decorate objects. They are associated subjects, but they differ technically. The basic difference is that marquetry is placed on a surface, and inlays are inserted into a surface.

Marquetry is the craft of cutting shapes from wooden veneers and laying them side by side to create the illusion of a pictorial subject. Inlaying is the craft of excavating a recess in a solid ground into which a smaller piece is inserted, or creating a shaped piece to fit into a recess.

Sometimes both techniques are combined; for example, after laying a marquetry picture on a board, it may be inlaid with a border to frame it. Or a motif produced by marquetry methods may then be inlaid into a solid ground, such as a decoration for a box lid.

Make no mistake, this form of adornment, at its tasteful best, belongs to the past. Its ancient origins are set in a time when such things were not only greatly prized, but were being produced by abundant artisans. But wait! The techniques are known to those preservers of precious practices who value the wholesome pleasure of creating this special ornamentation.

Earth's last renewable resource, wood, with its seemingly boundless service to man, has the amazing properties of both beauty and function. Combine these ingredients appropriately and mankind's relationship with nature is compounded in a most sublime way. Some of the craftsman's most satisfying moments will have been spent in the practice of shaping wood, an experience partially renewed each time the decorated article is brought out and displayed for appreciation by either an initiate or a master. This unique material is the vehicle that links the designer, the artist, the craftsman, the owner, and the admirer.

Without enlightenment there is mystery and, while the application of some of the most impressive decoration may appear to have been created by a genius, when the techniques are revealed it may be seen to be the attainable result of patient craftsmanship.

As your guide to the subject, I have described here various techniques accumu-lated during much of the last half century devoted to the study of specialized woodwork; they are intended to be of helpful inspiration rather than a rigid, definitive, method.

So, instead of looking wistfully at the crafts of yesteryear, convert the impetus of nostalgia into inspiration and speculate on the prospect of contributing your own skills to the enrich-ment of the future. It should be, after all, a gateway to our heritage and not a barrier.

I wish you great success and boundless joy from your endeavors, together with the hope that this book helps you attain them.

—*Zachary Taylor*

Part One: Marquetry

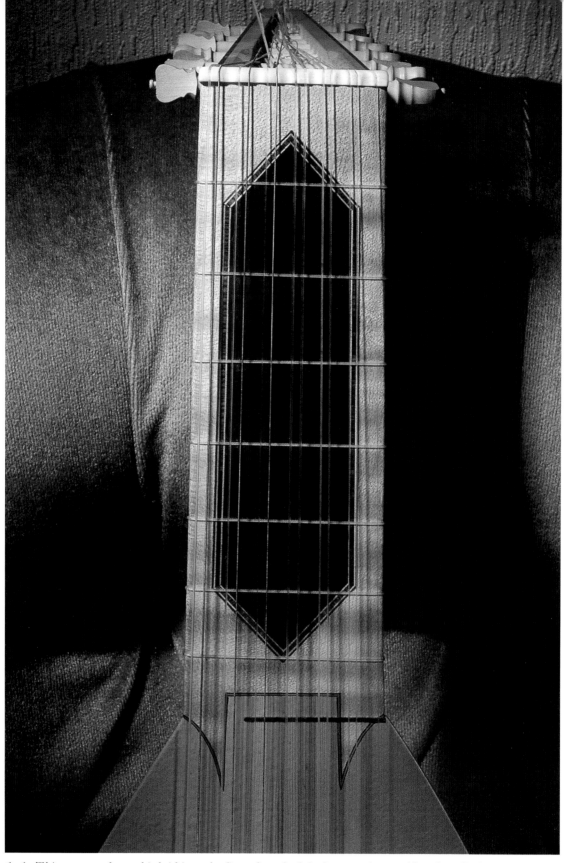

1–1. *This rosewood panel inlaid into the fingerboard of the lute can be considered applied marquetry.*

CHAPTER 1

INTRODUCTION TO MARQUETRY

Marquetry is the craft of cutting wood veneers to specific shapes and gluing them side by side to make patterns or pictures. Linguistically speaking, "marquetry" is taken from the word marqueterie and is used by the French for both overlaid and inlaid work. The word "intarsia" is also used widely to describe any kind of inlaid work, although in recent years, the term has been used to describe a distinct craft.

In considering definitions, a similar term, "parquetry," applies to the craft of arranging woods of different color in geometric patterns and laying them on a suitable surface. A near relative is the word "parquet," used to describe a similar technique, but using heavier pieces, normally to make an ornamental floor covering.

Veneers are the basic materials from which marquetry is created. It is usual to attach some artistic intention to the work, by the careful selection of the veneers. Variation in color and grain are what make up the marquetarian's palette. The marquetry craftsman may be referred to as a marqueter, marqueteur, or marquetarian, the last term having been chosen for this book.

Of the several ways to accomplish the precise cutting of the related parts, two basic techniques are common: by the knife, or by the saw. Decisions as to whether to use knife or saw will be partially decided by the type of veneer selected—thick or thin, in basic terms, meaning $\frac{1}{28}$th or $\frac{1}{40}$th of an inch, respectively. While the saw may be used for thick or thin veneers, only the thin type is applicable to knife cutting.

When the pieces have been cut to the

1–2. *An original pictorial marquetry piece, created by Jack Roseigh.*

required shape, they are assembled and mounted permanently on a rigid board, although it is most usual to cut the pieces and assemble them one at a time. It is normal to protect the surface with a suitable finish, such as varnish or wax. These techniques are dealt with in detail in later chapters.

PICTORIAL MARQUETRY

Pictorial marquetry is so-called to differentiate it from applied marquetry. In the former case, the intention is to create a complete, free-standing picture, and the latter refers to a decoration intended for application to another object. See Applied Marquetry below for more details.

Colors and grain patterns of wood veneers are the components and they may be seen as either limiting or inspiring, depending on the skills and the imagination of the marquetarian.

Marquetry pictures are often inspired by existing works of art, usually paintings, but occasionally they are original pieces produced specifically for marquetry **(1–2)**.

Suitable subjects for pictorial marquetry might be silhouettes, portraits, landscapes, still lifes, architectural scenes, abstract art, and so on.

Many commercial suppliers of marquetry products offer kits for beginners. Kits normally contain a design, a selection of veneers, even a knife, plus step-by-step instructions for the completion of a finished marquetry picture.

Applied Marquetry

Occasionally this takes the form of a marquetry motif representing some pattern or a pictorial scene, but if it is laid onto the surface of an object, it is generally said to be "applied," to differentiate it from a hang-on-the-wall marquetry picture (refer to photo on page 16). More often than not, it will be a geometric device, or border, applied to a box lid or some artifact. In some famous examples, whole cabinets and tabletops have been used as objects for applied marquetry. The French and Italian marquetarians of the past were particularly skillful in this craft.

Choosing the Subject
Aesthetics

Individual preferences will play the biggest part in this matter; in other words, is the subject interesting, inspiring, delightful, or in some other way attractive to the maker? Few people could enter into the prospect of spending time and energy on a project that lacked appeal to them personally. Added to this important element of personal aesthetics is the need to assess whether or not one has sufficient skill to cope with the technical requirements for a given example.

A beginner to marquetry might seek the safety of a kit for a start, in which case a choice of subject may be made by consulting catalogues. Suppliers usually classify them in grades of difficulty to help guide the marquetry student. Included in such a kit will be a full-size picture, often in color, together with a copy from which to work, and the required materials. Of course, the person who composes the kit will have made the choice of suitable materials and this selection might be a lesson in itself to the beginner. In time, the marquetry student should progress to the stage of creating a project from scratch.

If an existing picture is used as a marquetry subject, several issues must be considered before embarking on the project:

1. Is it important to try to create an accurate copy of the original or will an approximation suffice?

Bearing in mind that the range of natural wood colors is limited to browns, varying from pale creams to nearly black, with excursions into nearly red, color matching must be of primary consideration. For example, to attempt an accurate copy of Thomas Gainsborough's "The Blue Boy" would be ill advised!

2. If the color range demanded by the original is faithfully achievable with wood, what about the possible level of relevant detail? If the original is a painting, it should be realized that cutting techniques are not as precisely controllable, or as small, as brush strokes.

3. When considering a particular picture, does it carry a specific mood or tone that could be interpreted by the characteristics of wood grain?

4. Might it be sufficient to use a portion of a picture or to simplify some of its outlines to make the subjects more accessible as a marquetry project?

These are a few of the questions that the serious marquetarian must ask when contemplating the reproduction of any existing work.

Many pictures may provide inspiration for

a new creation or for a faithful reproduction, from postcards to prints of great paintings. There is an abundance of magazines, many containing excellent reproductions of art or photographs of natural scenes. Simple exercises such as silhouettes make an appropriate threshold project, especially as they are restricted to basic two-part designs and use only two contrasting colors.

It seems inevitable that some compromises must be made in translating from one medium to another, while trying to retain the integrity of the original subject, but that is one of the skills that the marquetarian needs to develop.

In many cases, the restricted color range of available woods can actually serve to enhance some subjects. Many painters are known to use a "limited palette" for that very reason. Using their skills in the use of tonal grading and subtle color mixing, it is possible to achieve a balanced and coordinated composition. Those seeking to excel in the origination of appropriate compositions are advised to try to develop that facility. It may be a self-imposed constraint by the painter, but it is the very nature of the marquetarian's palette.

Looking further into the needs of the subject in terms of interpretation of mood and tone, some discerning inspection of grain pattern is essential. A "quiet" subject might be shown very sensitively with lightly figured woods, whereas a dramatic picture might benefit from some highly flamed spectacular grain.

It is assumed in the foregoing that only natural wood colors are admissible. In all prob-

ability, supplies of dyed veneers will be obtainable from suppliers of marquetry products. This means an almost limitless range of colors are at the disposal of the marquetarian, but this is a resource that many regard as unacceptable. Color of natural wood or in an enhanced and artificial state is discussed in Chapter 3.

Different conditions apply to the creation of original work. To the artist or designer, marquetry may represent a splendid opportunity to express some idea or a novel approach to an artistic statement. With experience, marquetarians can combine acquired practical skills and their creative abilities with the natural qualities exclusive to wood. These may provide the opportunity to exploit the subject fully in all aspects while incorporating the individual's artistic values. An artist who may be accustomed to producing line drawings, for example, may easily create this type of work using marquetry principles. Lines enclosing areas in the drawing might be seen to be represented by cutting with a knife or by saw blade. It follows that smooth flowing lines are followed by the knife or saw more effectively than sharp turns or interrupted detail. Enclosed areas may be recognized as separate fields to be filled with veneer.

With luck, exhibitions may be given by nearby marquetry societies, or perhaps museums with examples of ancient furniture with veneered ornamentation. Newcomers to the craft will quickly form opinions as to which types of work appeal most and, happily, this should lead to some constructive guidance in their development as marquetarians.

CHAPTER 2

COPYING THE PICTURE

Having decided on the subject for the marquetry project, the process of selection should proceed as suggested in the previous chapter. Assuming that any amendments necessary have been made, a copy must be produced. Depending on the technique to be used in the cutting of the component parts of the picture, the copy should be on either plain paper or transparent film. Technical reasons for this are explained in the chapters dealing with the applications of knife and saw. Either way, the principles of making a copy are similar. Bearing in mind that veneers often come in small pieces, the size of the working pattern may be critical. Comparison of measurements between the original and the available veneers should readily determine the correct size of the copy. It may be necessary to reduce the original to a smaller scale to accommodate the selected materials. Various methods of copying and scaling are detailed below.

ENLARGING OR REDUCING WITH A GRID

A grid is drawn on the pattern, and a corresponding grid is drawn to the required scale for the copy (2–1). Where the lines of the pattern intersect with its grid, marks are made correspondingly on the copy. It is then a simple matter to join up the dots.

COPYING WITH A PANTOGRAPH

Designs can be copied at various scales, depending on the arrangement of the pantograph arms. In 2–2, the tracing point follows the outline of the design and the pencil draws an enlarged copy.

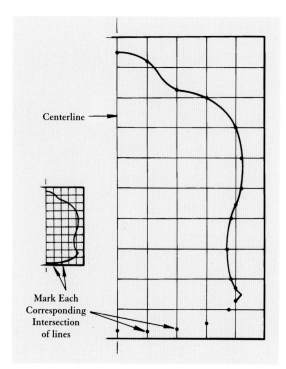

Centerline

Mark Each
Corresponding
Intersection
of lines

2–1. *Enlarging or reducing with a grid. For a rough-and-ready copy, or if no other method is available, a satisfactory copy may be produced by grid reference. It is not a very quick or accurate method of detailed copying, but, if required, refinements can be added after the basic design has been transferred.*

If the original is disposable, a grid of squares is drawn on the picture. A specific measurement is used, such as 1-inch divisions. On a piece of paper intended for the copy, a corresponding grid is drawn, made up of bigger squares to enlarge the copy, or smaller squares to reduce it. If the original measures, say, 4 x 6 inches and the desired copy will increase to 8 x 12 inches, then the grid on the copy will be drawn with 2-inch squares. It helps if the grid lines are numbered.

It may be important to preserve the original without damage. To achieve this, a transparent film can be prepared, with a grid inscribed in ink and laid over the original. The picture can be seen through the transparent film, and where any line of its features crosses a grid line, it can be marked and transferred to the copy.

PHOTOCOPYING

Most people have access to a photocopier, belonging to an office, public library, or print shop. If the original work is in public domain, or out of copyright, one is free to make copies. Where copyright material is concerned, permission must be obtained from those in ownership before copies may be made. Fortunately, so much unencumbered material is available that formal permission to copy generally is not needed. In this case, no infringement of the law is perpetrated, since the purpose of the copy is merely as a reference, with no intention of using the copy for financial gain.

The major advantage of the modern photocopier is its facility to make enlargements or reductions from an original. Most photocopiers print in black and white, this being perfectly satisfactory for the purpose of a marquetry pattern. Another facility of the modern machine is that it incorporates control of light exposure to give darker or lighter prints. It is possible to print copies in black and white from colored originals. This can be an advantage in two respects: 1, tonal graduations are well defined; and 2, outlines of features are more easily discernible. In any case, it is unlikely that the colors contained in the original picture could be matched accurately, unless it was itself a marquetry picture! Even then, exact duplication would be almost impossible.

COPYING BY COMPUTER PROCESSING

Recently, it has been possible to connect photographic image scanners to personal computers. Scanners come in several forms to facilitate the transfer of images from photographic prints, slides, or negatives into the computer.

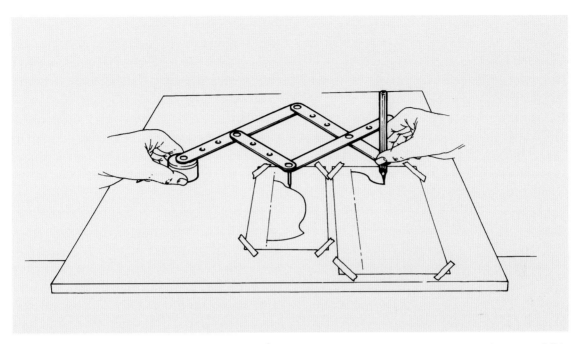

2–2. *Copies can be made with a pantograph, an ancient device for enlarging or reducing drawings. This drawing tool is a four-piece frame whose pivoted arms may be assembled in variable positions to change the scale of the drawing. One end of the frame acts as an anchor remaining fixed in one position during the copying procedure. A pencil is fixed at the other end and is used to draw the outline of the subject. The central part of the frame forms a parallelogram, the lower corner of which carries a point, to act as a tracer. As the tracer is guided to follow the design, the pencil draws a copy, either larger, smaller, or the same size, depending on the arrangement of the arms of the frame.*

Some care is required initially to locate the picture and the copy paper, both of which should be attached temporarily, to avoid movement during the tracing operation. Before starting to trace, the pantograph should be contracted to its minimum, with the base secured, if possible. With the pantograph in this position, the original picture should be located with its lower left corner beneath the tracing point. Tape or pins should be used to secure the picture. When the copy paper is positioned, its sides must be parallel to those of the picture. The pencil on the pantograph must be located at the lower left corner of the copy paper to correspond with the position of the tracer on the original picture. It takes a little experience to control the movement of the pantograph arms to produce a good copy, but it is a worthwhile skill to develop, as it has many applications.

Scanned images can be manipulated by software installed in the computer's operating system, and then printed. In those few sentences lies an enormous complexity of technology, far beyond the scope of this book or this author! Suffice it to say that it is possible to learn to use all of the aforementioned apparatus with a few instructions from a friendly computer guru. If such a facility is not available through social connections, many commercial print shops can perform the same service. Virtually limitless possibilities are at the disposal of the experienced operator, including the production of a marquetry look-alike!

This is still only one of the steps, of course, in the making of the pattern on which the marquetry picture is to be based.

THE WORKING PATTERN

As was stated earlier, either the photocopier or the printer will deliver prints on plain white paper, from which the pattern can be transcribed. This might be produced as a simple tracing using carbon paper for the transfer, as follows: Lay down a piece of white paper slightly larger than the pattern and cover it with carbon paper, print side down. Over this place the copy of the original and keep all three sheets together on a work board with masking tape. Trace over the outlines of the elements of the picture with a scribing tool or a ballpoint pen. The latter has the benefit of leaving a mark showing which elements have been outlined. It is also an opportunity to adjust the pattern, such as smoothing out some of the sharp corners, or leaving out some undesirable features. Maybe some detail is added here and there for the sake of the picture "story." This is the point at which the picture is composed, and some tests might be well advised. After all, it is easy enough to create several copies for trial runs before starting to cut veneers.

It may be advantageous to use a copy produced on tracing paper or transparent film. The latter, being more durable than paper, is used by draftsmen from which to make copies. It is ideal for the marquetarian, too, particularly as the veneers may be viewed and selected through the traced copy. Tracings on drafting film may be made by hand-applied pen and ink or by a computer-driven printer.

CHAPTER 3

WOOD VENEERS

Wood veneer comes in wafer-thin sheets peeled from logs on a machine that resembles a huge pencil sharpener. In the process, an "inside" and an "outside" of the veneer are produced (3–1), one side with the grain more open than the other. Generally, one side will be smooth and the other somewhat rougher. It is best to plan to use the smooth side for the face of the design. It is easy to recognize which is which by flexing a sample (3–2 and 3–3). A slight tendency to curve may well be seen if the veneer is laid on a flat surface, and this tendency may be encouraged with a little help by flexing it with the fingers.

The description "wafer-thin" requires quantifying and this differs according to which side of the Atlantic is being considered, there being no global standard. In America,

the manufactured standard thickness is $\frac{1}{28}$th of an inch (about .9 mm), whereas in Europe veneers are nominally $\frac{1}{40}$ inch (.6 or .7 mm; both thicknesses are available).

For the sake of easy comparison, American veneer is 1½ times thicker than

3–1. *In the above example, a small sheet of veneer is seen to have a slight curve across the grain. This shows the upper side, or the "outside" of the piece.*

3–2. *If encouraged carefully, and, as long as the test is carried out with caution, it is possible to increase the curve without damage, as may be seen in the illustration.*

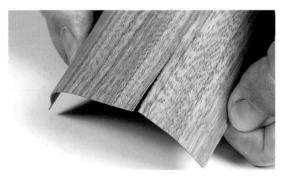

3–3. *Attempts to curve the same example in the opposite direction, in effect, to try to turn it inside out, results in failure and cracking. In cases where marquetry is intended for application to a curved object, such as a box lid, this feature of veneer is best considered at the planning stage.*

European veneer. In practical terms, this means that because of the inherent difficulty in cutting the thicker veneers with the knife, especially the hardwoods, marquetry in the United States is most commonly cut with a saw. The availability of thinner veneers in Europe offers the choice of cutting with knife or saw. To generalize, European marquetarians, professional and amateur, use the saw and amateurs use the knife; this is especially so for the British. In fact, the majority of British marquetry is done with the knife, simply because there are far more amateurs than professionals.

It would be a mistake to conclude from this that one method is superior to the other. Both techniques have their pros and cons and there are examples in which both are capable of producing results of a quality indistinguishable from each other.

It is true that sawing represents speed, particularly if the Boulle technique is used, involving the cutting of multiple layers. Sawing may also achieve detailed working of stubborn hardwoods that cause problems with knife cutting. However, there is something enormously appealing about the use of the knife, with its simplicity and economic use of tools and materials. A sense of rustic homeliness, of firesides and comfort, with a work board on the knee attracts many to this method. One great advantage with knife cutting using the "window" technique (more on this later) is that the veneer proposed to fill a particular aperture may be viewed through that aperture prior to cutting it. This advantage enables the marquetarian to adjust for maximum effect before cutting the veneer.

It is not surprising that the word "marquetry" is French (from "marqueter," meaning to inlay), considering that the most famous center for the craft is in Paris. The École Boulle, which was founded by André-Charles Boulle, one of the most highly respected veneer artists, still uses his sawing techniques.

Although veneer of any thickness may be sawn, it would not be wise to mix veneer thicknesses in one piece of work, because at the finishing stage the whole surface must be leveled. An uneven surface would almost certainly risk the hazard of rubbing through the thinner sections to reveal portions of the baseboard on which the marquetry was mounted.

Leaving aside, for the moment, the question of thickness, consider the other characteristics of wood veneer that affect the marquetarian. Foremost is the color, or, in other words, the palette, mentioned earlier in Choosing the Subject (pages 19 and 20).

In creating an attainable color chart, it should be emphasized that variety is one of nature's gifts. It is also true to say that just when it is felt that a reliable knowledge of a particular wood is secure, along comes a sample of a different color, or grain pattern. So, while it is good to have a mental picture of the color of a species, or even a collection of samples for reference, no surprises should be expected if some variations are encountered. Generally, when choosing colors, it is advisable to visit the veneer supplier, if possible, to see exactly what is available. Again it must be stressed that the characteristics of individual specimens can vary from the norm, even within one piece of veneer. Often as not on such a visit, other varieties will be noticed and these can lead to further possibilities, perhaps even a fresh idea for a new color scheme.

As yet, there has been no mention of artificial coloring of veneers. This is a very controversial matter. Many marquetarians object to the use of dyed veneers, suggesting that one might just as well take up painting. Others see the use of artificial color as a means of expressing more fully the artistic potential of the craft. The author restricts his choice to the use of natural woods with the following concessions: reducing color intensity of a veneer by treating it with bleach or by darkening it with hot sand. More details of these methods appear in Changing Veneer Colors on pages 28 to 32. Many may find this an accept-

able method of enhancement, as no dye or artificial coloring is used to alter the basic color of the veneer. It must always be a matter for individual taste, unless, as stated earlier, some association or perhaps a competition imposes specific rules concerning the use of color.

Speaking of rules, a marquetry group with healthy numbers may launch a competition with ten or more classes, each of which will have specific features to include in the entered work—such as size of marquetry, numbers of veneers to use, and whether the classes are accessible to previous winners, or whether they are exclusive to those who have never won a prize, etc.

Apart from the color of the veneer, a valuable characteristic that contributes much to the pictorial quality of the work is grain patterns. These may be described variously as "straight," "wavy," "interlocked," "irregular," "spiral," "flamed," "quilted," or "fiddleback," with some dramatic excursions into "burrs" and "curls." Often as not, if an opportunity occurs to browse through a supplier's veneer stock, some piece will leap out at random with some immediate appeal. A whole picture can be inspired by just one veneer leaf bearing some unusual feature of hue or grain. Knowing this, the marquetarian will find the possibility of "serendipity" irresistible if suddenly confronted by a stack of veneers.

When identifying the veneer by name, it is more reliable to refer to a species by its Latin name, due to variations of common terms from country to country. For example, the wood known as sycamore to Americans would appear in a British catalogue as London plane, or lacewood, if cut to reveal a lace-like pattern.

Texture among woods in terms of its physical structure differs greatly from coarse and fibrous to dense and smooth, some soft and some hard. Each will make its own demands at the cutting stage, but whatever difficulties have to be overcome should not be discernible in the finished piece, with its smoothed and polished surface.

CHANGING VENEER COLORS

Many reject the idea of applying dye or other artificial means to change colors of wood, reasoning that one might as well simply apply paint to make whatever color is desired—in which case, if color is the only criterion, the use of wood may be rejected altogether, in favor of painting pictures. Others, like the author, prefer to apply bleach for lightening, or heat for darkening, to achieve a change, by a few shades, in the wood's natural color. For those who accept this, the following techniques are recommended.

Bleaching

Ordinary household bleach, used with discretion (either diluted or undiluted), has the effect of reducing the color intensity of most material, including wood. Often, the process is used to lighten pale woods to achieve as near white as possible. Some species bleach readily and others take more time. Tests are advised in every case, using spare material, if available.

Assuming that the most convenient method uses domestic bleach, the following simple procedure should produce a satisfactory result: Wearing a pair of rubber gloves, pour a little bleach into a nonmetallic container and set aside the resealed bleach bottle. With a nylon brush, apply the bleach to the surface of the veneer and watch for the effect of the

bleaching action. Alternatively, the wood may be immersed in the bleach and set aside to dry.

It is possible to isolate portions of the workpiece for the bleaching treatment, to produce a variegated or even a graduated effect.

Several treatments may be necessary to achieve the required reduction in color intensity, following which the wood should be washed thoroughly and left to dry.

Darkening with Heated Sand

Darkening veneer is a process used for creating the illusion of shading, usually to create the illusion of a contour in an area that might otherwise appear to be flat or featureless. The following is a traditional technique that offers rapid results with excellent control. The equipment needed includes a metal saucepan, a portable gas heater, a jar containing fine sand, extra-long matches, tweezers, and a small spoon (3–4).

A metal container is filled with fine sand to a depth of about an inch and placed on a heat source, such as a gas or electric heater (3–5 and 3–6). Samples may be tested when the sand is heated sufficiently; normally, it takes just a few moments. It is best to hold smaller samples in a pair of tweezers to avoid accidentally burning the fingers.

Experimentation is essential to determine to what depth and for how long the veneer should be inserted (3–7 and 3–8). The deeper the insertion, the greater the area of scorching that results. Deeper insertions may be necessary with larger pieces, but quite large areas may be scorched by plunging the veneer into the sand at a low angle. Some woods are more

Text Continues on Page 32

DARKENING VENEER

3–4. *Equipment for the hot-sand treatment to darken veneers: metal saucepan; portable gas heater; jar containing fine sand; extra-long matches; tweezers; a small spoon.*

3–5. *From the glass jar, sand is poured into the saucepan to a depth of about 1 inch (25 mm).*

3–6. *Using a long safety match, the gas burner is lit.*

DARKENING VENEER (continued)

3–7. *Waste veneer may be used to test the sand temperature, and when it is hot enough to scorch, the process of darkening can begin.*

3–8. *Most often, the darkening is required to produce a graduated, shaded, effect. This is achieved by immersing in the sand the part to be darkened and withdrawing it progressively as the scorching develops.*

3–9. *When the technique is learned, it is possible to try a more refined project intended for inlaying or marquetry.*

DARKENING VENEER (continued)

3–10. *Great care is exercised to control the time and depth of the immersion, especially since, as shown here, the point of the piece may easily be burnt.*

3–11. *Withdrawal can be made at various stages of the process to inspect the scorched area until a satisfactory effect is achieved.*

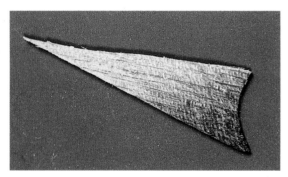

3–12. *A small part of a design intended to be made up eventually into a marquetry motif for inlaying.*

3–13. *Preparing to scorch an isolated portion, in this case a circle. A covering sheet with the hole acts like a stencil and beneath it is the veneer intended for scorching.*

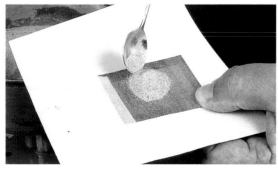

3–14. *Hot sand is taken from the saucepan in a spoon and poured onto the stencil.*

3–15. *Scorching has been limited to the area exposed by the stencil. It may be darkened with further applications if required.*

DARKENING VENEER (continued)

3–16. *The shaded piece.*

heat-resistant than others, so precise information as to timing is impossible. Overscorching of the wood should be avoided, because the burnt surface may crack and flake away, ruining the material beyond redemption. With a little practice, it is feasible to graduate the scorching effect to produce very subtle changes of tone **(3–9** to **3–12)**. If it is necessary to restrict the shading to one isolated area, this is possible by gluing, temporarily, a portion of veneer over the area to be unaffected.

Some difficulties may be experienced with the shading of large pieces or portions difficult to access. These problems may be overcome by pouring the hot sand from a spoon over the area to be shaded. If it is necessary to shade an area surrounded by unscorched veneer, such as a dark circle in the center of a pale patch, it may be produced thus: From waste veneer, cut a piece to cover the item to be shaded. Cut from the waste an aperture of the size and in the place of the intended area for scorching. Fix the two veneers together temporarily, with glue, tape, or tweezers **(3–13)**. Pour the heated sand to cover the aperture in the waste veneer **(3–14)** and wait a few seconds. Tip away the sand to reveal the scorched area and judge what degree of scorching is needed **(3–15)**. Obviously, the longer the heated sand stays in contact, the more the wood will scorch and the darker will be the result **(3–16)**.

CHAPTER 4

KNIVES AND OTHER EQUIPMENT

INTRODUCTION

With reference to veneer thickness, as detailed in the chapter Wood Veneers, the use of the knife for marquetry is normally limited to the cutting of materials of up to $\frac{1}{40}$ inch. To the European, this translates as thicknesses of .6 or .7 mm, both of which are readily obtainable in Europe, and increasingly so in America. These thicknesses may not always be available worldwide, so some research may be necessary to source local supplies.

Knives come in various shapes and sizes, giving some opportunity for individual choice, but some principles are applicable if best results are to be achieved. Perhaps it is unnecessary to suggest that a slender, but strong, blade is desirable, with a comfortable handle. General-purpose craft knives are often too heavy-bladed for the refined application demanded of marquetry, and lightweight scalpel blades are too flexible to give the necessary control.

Knives designed especially for marquetry by marquetarians, and made by specialized manufacturers, are best, of course, and worth acquiring.

Sharpness is the foremost essential and it is this quality that diminishes with each stroke. Constant attention to the cutting edge is therefore a built-in process accompanying every successful project. It may be assumed that a sharpening hone must accompany the acquisition of the knife. Details of hones and sharpening are given later in this chapter.

Control of the knife is something that is acquired gradually with experience, but familiarity with correct technique can be encouraged from the start. Angles of cutting and penetration must be developed conscientiously and with discipline. With the formation of good technique, the powers of concentration can be directed toward the aesthetic content of the work. The same would apply to artists who, having had sufficient practice and experience, can mix their paints or draw lines instinctively.

A basic kit of tools and equipment follows; it is by no means extensive, but is sufficient to get going on a first project.

KNIVES

Knives are obtainable from marquetry suppliers in some variety and, happily, they all work (4–1). Undoubtedly, given trials with different knife designs, individual preferences will be forthcoming.

Craft Knives

Designed and developed especially for modeling and associated uses, the craft knife usually comes with detachable blades in a comfortable handle (4–2 to 4–12). Blade designs are similar to the scalpel with additional variations. Some manufacturers offer a selection of handles with a complementary range of blades, including saws and carving tools. For the marquetarian who has wide

4–1. A range of knives, some for general craft application and others intended for marquetry.

CRAFT KNIVES

4–2. This knife has a robust handle into which may be inserted various blades and even small chisels and gouges. It is good for general-purpose modeling as well as marquetry.

4–3. Changing blades on this knife requires the unscrewing of a collar to release or retain the blade.

4–4. A screwdriver is needed to open this knife handle.

CRAFT KNIVES (continued)

4–5. *When the screw is undone, the handle separates into two parts for removal or replacement of the blade.*

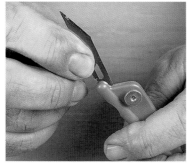

4–6. *An inexpensive, general-purpose knife with good marquetry application. The lightweight handle has firm support of the blade. Due to the short blade projection, care must be taken when changing blades.*

4–7. *A pair of tweezers is advised to assist in handling.*

4–8. *Designed by Ernie Ives, this knife is a popular marquetry tool, with its slender handle and delicate blade.*

4–9. *Changing blades requires the unscrewing of the lower part of the handle.*

4–10. *Removal or replacement of blades is best done with the help of a pair of tweezers.*

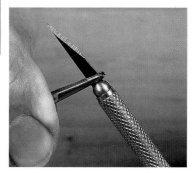

4–11. *The author's favorite marquetry knife, with a slender blade in a knurled, easy-grip, handle. It has excellent control and is comfortable to hold for long periods.*

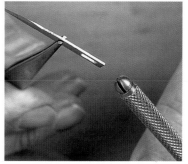

4–12. *Unscrewing of the knurled section releases the blade for changing.*

woodworking interests, the craft knife may have a special appeal.

Snap-Off Blades

Not dedicated especially to marquetry, these tools come in a slim handle with a sliding, retractable blade. The blade stock is scored at regular intervals, allowing the end to be broken off when worn, to access a new, unused portion. An unusual feature is the sharpened edge; being a snap-off design, it is on the lower side of the

SNAP-OFF BLADES

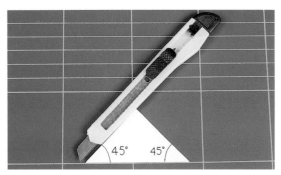

4–13. *This photograph shows how, when the snap-off cutting edge is at 45 degrees, the leading edge is past the vertical, reducing penetration of the blade.*

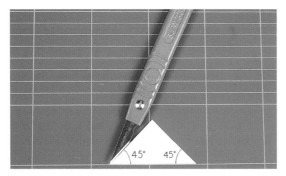

4–14. *With its edge at 45 degrees, the leading edge of the replaceable blade is less than 90 degrees, making penetration easier and therefore less stressful, with greater ease when tracking curves.*

blade in line with the handle. Unfortunately, the angle of the knife point is greater than the marquetry knife and this adversely affects its penetration **(4–13** and **4–14).**

Note: Surgical scalpels are inexpensive, high-specification, tools. They are exceptionally sharp and resist blunting better than most, but their relatively thin blades are very flexible, with a tendency to follow the grain rather than a prescribed line.

CUTTING MAT

A cutting mat is made from semi-hard laminated plastic with a so-called "self-healing" surface **(4–15).** Provided that the cutting is restricted to normal marquetry techniques, the surface remains undamaged even after the production of many pieces of work. The cutting mat does represent a somewhat expensive investment, so its acquisition might be delayed until a later stage. Several sizes are available; best to go for the next size up from the one that is suitable at the moment, because usually one's ambition expands!

A suitable alternative is a vinyl floor tile; it costs next-to-nothing and gives good service.

CUTTING MAT

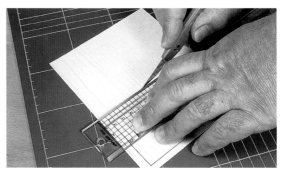

4–15. *A straightedge, in use as a cutting guide as shown here, resting on a cutting mat.*

STRAIGHTEDGE

If the marquetry budget allows, the best straightedges are made of stainless steel to avoid rusting and thick enough to remain rigid if used as a cutting guide (refer to **4–15**).

A rigid rule, made from transparent plastic, calibrated for measuring, and incorporating a steel edge to act as a cutting guide, is also a practical multipurpose implement.

COMBINATION SQUARE

A combination square is needed for checking right angles, square lines, and miter angles on frames. The conventional engineering type is most useful and serves many purposes, including that of a cutting guide in certain applications.

TWEEZERS

Two kinds are needed: one pair of the open-ended type that close when squeezed, and the other pair that open when squeezed (refer to **4–7** and **4–10**). The latter serves as a temporary lightweight clamp while gluing together small pieces.

WORK BOARD

This is to replace a work top or a bench and, although its function is to serve as an alternative to both, it could be placed on top of any sturdy surface. It is recommended to use plastic-faced particleboard, in white or some other pale color. Portability and storage are benefits of this material along with its clean, smooth surface. One approximately 2 feet square (approximately 600 mm square) should be ample for the job, and almost any do-it-yourself store should be able to supply this, cut to size if need be. Many of the illustrations used throughout this book are photographed on such a work board.

Numerous other aids and devices will be necessary as the work progresses, but most may be accumulated gradually, with little need to search beyond the kitchen or woodshed.

ADHESIVES

In the world of the woodworker, there has never been so wide a choice of adhesives. However, modern adhesives lack the most important feature of the traditional, animal glues: it is not easy, and in some cases it is impossible, to reverse modern glues.

Some glues recently available may be released with the application of an agent to soften the set adhesive, but it almost certainly cannot be reactivated and there are problems removing it from the wood in preparation for its replacement. In contrast, the old hide glue concoctions made from boiling fish bones, rabbit skin, sinews, etc., are not only releasable after setting, but may be reactivated and are therefore reusable, just by the application of heat or hot water.

Today, traditional animal glues may be acquired from appropriate suppliers in granular form, requiring soaking in water to soften them. Heating the glue will then create a mixture of glue and water, variable in consistency according to the user's preference. It should be thin enough to apply to the joint with a brush, somewhat like thin varnish. In any kind of situation where separation is required of glued joints, animal glue has no superior. A happy alternative, particularly where small amounts are needed, is liquid hide glue. It comes in a convenient bottle and needs no preparation other than to remove the top and tip it out. It is reversible and behaves very much like hot glue.

Other more commonplace adhesives such as caseins, polyvinyl acetates (PVA's), aliphatics, epoxy resins, etc., may be used for marquetry and inlaying and are readily available at every hardware or woodwork store.

Part of the gluing process is securing the parts while the adhesive dries, or cures, and for this, several means are available. For holding down veneered panels such as marquetry pictures, clamps may be used or pressure applied with weights. The clamps should have plastic pressure pads attached to the clamping surfaces, to avoid bruising the veneer. Small pieces may be held with adhesive tape.

Most importantly, the setting time must be observed fastidiously and 25 percent added to the time recommended by the manufacturer, to err on the safe side. After all, it took long enough to create the masterpiece and patience requires no skill at all.

SHARPENING KNIVES AND OTHER TOOLS

If a prioritized list were drawn up of all the skills needed in the craft of woodwork that contribute by their virtues, or obstruct by their faults, sharpening would appear at the top. No matter how skilled the operator, no matter how experienced in technical know-how, if the tools are defective, the work will suffer.

Most will have heard the saying that "it is a poor workman who blames his tools." However, an experienced woodworker should blame the tools if they are deficient and either exchange them or improve them, whichever is more appropriate. In the case of edge tools, improvement usually means making them sharper.

Sharpening ought not to be regarded as a chore, but the essential prerequisite to the craftsman's first step toward high-quality work. It seems that those who least enjoy the sharpening process are those who have not learned the skills it requires. Obviously, it is better to be shown the techniques by an experienced guide, rather than to try to learn from a book or video, and that is what I recommend. Most qualified tutors of cabinetwork or joinery are likely to be able to teach tool sharpening because the principles involved will be common to all aspects of the craft.

As to equipment required to sharpen edge tools, there is a wide choice. In the past, an enthusiast's kit might comprise a collection of hones ranging from very coarse Carborundum grit through slate, natural Arkansas and Wichita stones and leather. Nowadays it might be represented by a combination of Japanese water stones, diamond hones, and ceramic stones, varying in grit from about 1,000 to 8,000. For exceptionally sharp edges, it is still difficult to beat the stropping of a scalpel with leather, if very fine work is needed. At the coarse end of the subject, a double-ended bench grinder will remove hefty waste very quickly, if fundamental reshaping of blades is necessary.

SHARPENING WITH HONES

Ideally the marquetry tool kit will contain at least two hones, commonly still called "stones," even if they are no longer actually made of stone (4–16). For honing the sharp edge of a blade, a hard, fine-grade type is best, such as a diamond or ceramic hone; pocket size is sufficient. The so-called "diamond" hone is made of a metal base whose surface is covered in diamond particles, and the ceramic stone is a composition of alumina in a hard synthetic ceramic paste. Both are more expensive than natural materials such as Wichita or Arkansas stones, although even these cost more than the common Carborundum type.

Each hone imposes its own technique—

with or without lubricant, and, if so, what kind of lubricant, and so on. Recommendations of the manufacturer should be followed. Ceramics and diamond-coated hones are appealing because a little water is all that is required to lubricate them, whereas most of the old stones needed an oily lubricant as a grinding agent. Few would willingly introduce cutting oils into a woodworking environment.

If operating on an austere budget, it is acceptable to use an alternative to shop-bought hones, for example, an abrasive sheet glued to a piece of flat material such as medium-density fiberboard. Several grades of abrasive may be applied to shop-made hones ranging from, say, 240 to about 1,000 grit. Shop-made hones may be shaped according to individual requirements and should not be regarded as inferior, since they perform very well and offer considerable savings. If they are relatively small, they may be operated with one hand holding the blade and the other applying the hone. The blade may then be moved across the steady hone or vice versa. From fine silica papers to very fine abrasives like Micromesh, the hones may be made to individual specifications.

Bench stones operate better if fixed in some way to prevent movement during the sharpening process. Some brands are supplied in a box with nonskid feet. A sturdy, stable surface is required to support the stone since the effort of sharpening has the propensity to move the stone forward and back, an obviously undesirable liability.

Illus. **4–17** to **4–19** show how to sharpen blades with a hone.

Another way of "sharpening" is to grind away the worn point of a blade to reach an unused portion of the blade (**4–20**). A common Carborundum hone is sufficient for the job.

SHARPENING WITH HONES

4–16. *A marquetry knife on the far left, and, from left to right, hones: a natural slip stone; a ceramic hone, double-sided, with medium and fine grit; a diamond hone in a folding handle; a small diamond hone; and a Japanese water stone.*

This is not, strictly speaking, sharpening, but it has a similar effect in that it removes the blunt edge to access an unused portion of the blade. However, it does change the blade's angle at its point and wears it away more rapidly than the conventional method of sharpening.

Illus. **4–21** shows a useful hone made from sheet material, faced on either side with suitable abrasives, usually of different grits.

TYPES OF KNIFE BLADES

Knife blades vary in design from thin to broad in section, from parallel to tapered, from pointed to rounded and from straight-edged to curved. Most marqueterians and inlayers have a collector's attitude to tools, particularly to knives, with the result that there are usually more blades in the kit than are actually needed; but it's not a bad thing to have a choice, providing it doesn't become obsessive.

Reducing the blade's thickness by beveling each side produces a cutting edge. Marquetry knives will require beveling at about 5 degrees on each side, and it is easy to make a guide to

SHARPENING KNIFE BLADES WITH A HONE

4–17. *Sharpening a blade is a matter of applying a disciplined technique, the principles of which are maintaining a fixed angle at a consistent pressure while rubbing the blade along the surface of the hone.*

4–18. *The commencement of the stroke is with the bevel, not the flat of the blade, resting on the surface of the hone. Here the operator is halfway through the stroke, with the angle of the blade and pressure consistent. It is important not to wobble the knife during the movement.*

4–19. *Completion of the stroke, and the bevel is still in contact with the surface of the hone. Several passes may be needed to bring a blunt blade back to perfection, but the more regularly it is done, the less work is required with the hone and the better will be the cutting operation.*

SHARPENING KNIFE BLADES WITH A HONE (continued)

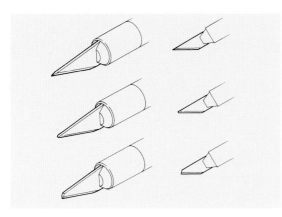

4–20. *Above are examples showing, on the left, three conditions of blade points. Top: A correctly sharp blade point. Center: The same blade, but the point is rounded from wear. Bottom: The blade after grinding back the point to provide a new, sharp cutting edge. While not pointed, it will serve for many applications in this rejuvenated shape.*

4–21. *A useful hone made from sheet material, faced on either side with suitable abrasives, usually of different grits. If operating on an austere budget, it is acceptable to use an alternative to shop-bought hones, for example, an abrasive sheet glued to a piece of flat material, such as medium-density fiberboard. Several grades of abrasive may be applied to shop-made hones ranging from about 240 to 1,000 grit. Shop-made hones may be shaped according to individual requirements and should not be regarded as inferior, since they perform very well and offer considerable savings. If they are relatively small they may be operated with one hand holding the blade and the other applying the hone. The blade may then be moved across the steady hone or vice versa. From fine silica papers to very fine abrasives like Micromesh, the hones may be made to individual requirements.*

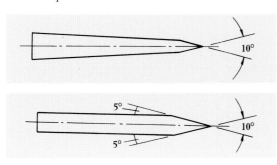

4-22.

check this by cutting out a V-shaped gap of 10 degrees in a piece of cardboard (**4–22**). The top illustration shows a parallel-thickness blade, typical of most disposable craft knives. Below it is a tapered-thickness blade, normally found in more robust, fixed-blade knives. The recommended bevel is the same for both types.

It is probably sufficient to draw a bevel angle with a protractor to use as a visual guide with which to compare the appearance of the beveled edge as it is being created.

If using craft knives of the variety found with disposable blades, it is better if the knife incorporates a clamping device, to ensure that the blade is fixed securely to the handle. Any tendency for the blade to move, during either marking or incising, may nullify the operation.

Implicit to the term "disposable" is the suggestion that the blunted blade is redundant, and, therefore, discardable. However, it is possible to sharpen even a scalpel blade virtually to its original pristine condition—many times, before replacement becomes necessary. This is helped by the fact that these types of blades are made from parallel sections and may be rejuvenated almost to extinction. Tapered blades present a thicker section as the edge is sharpened, and need reforming on a bench grinder when the thinner part of the blade has been worn away.

An extreme example of a thick section reduced to a fine cutting edge is an old-fashioned cut-throat razor. The reduction in the blade thickness is in fact not a bevel but a concave radius brought to an unimaginably fine edge. Its brutal name, while pejorative, is nonetheless descriptive, but hopefully the marqueterian will see more creative uses for it. Cut-throat razors may be bought in sophisticated barbershops, or, perhaps more appealing to our imaginative craftsman, they often turn up in second-hand shops at prices less than 10 percent of the new price—even less, if the edge is badly serrated or the end broken off, rendering them useless for shaving. For our purpose, these deficiencies do not matter as they will be ground away to create our custom-shaped blade. Epoxy adhesive may be used to fix the blade shaft into a new wooden handle, predrilled to accommodate it. There are endless possibilities, but this is not the place to detail them further.

Blades intended for chip carving and the like are suitable for some marquetry operations providing they are not overthick, due to the need to cut into our ground with minimal width of cut. These blades may be tapered in section, already partly beveled from the back to the edge, requiring a secondary bevel to be applied to sharpen it. The same angular considerations are recommended as to the parallel blade detailed above.

SHARPENING KNIFE BLADES

Applying a blade at the first stage of sharpening, the back edge of the blade (nearest the body) is raised to bring the bevel flat on the stone. The grinding action is produced as the blade is pushed away (4–23).

On completion of the return stroke, it is necessary to rotate the blade to bring the opposite face in contact with the stone (4–24). To achieve this, the blade is rotated to keep the back of the blade in contact with the stone, not the sharp edge. Alternatively, in rotating the blade it may be removed from contact with the stone to avoid contacting the stone surface with the sharp edge. The blade is then pulled toward the body with the opposite bevel in contact with the stone, still with the sharp edge leading the stroke, and now facing the operator.

SHARPENING BLADES FOR CHANNEL CUTTERS

The channel cutter is used for marking or cutting channels* for the inlay of purfling. Its job is to mark or incise with a small blade fitted to a device that incorporates a fence, or guide, permitting an incision to be made parallel with a straight or curved edge. If the blades are shop-made, or if the blade in the proprietary cutter is lost or worn out, replacement is straightforward. Most craftsmen will have access to broken hacksaw blades—if not from one's own workshop, then a polite request at almost any car-repair shop should bear fruit. One hacksaw blade will provide enough blades to last a lifetime. A bench

* A channel is a square-sided recess with a section of material removed. It is wider than a groove.

grinder is essential for this task—to first form the end of the hacksaw blade to the required shape prior to parting it off. It is also easier to hone the edge to sharpness before separating it from the main saw blade.

Blades for the channel cutter are different from knife blades because they have a bevel on only one side of the blade but on both edges (**4–25**). This is to permit cutting in both directions along a periphery, while leaving one side of the cut perfectly square to the face of the ground. This ensures a close fit of the inlay, whereas, theoretically, a beveled edge will produce a slightly angled channel side.

SHARPENING SCRAPER BLADES

At least two types of scrapers are normal to our marquetry workshop, with variations in

SHARPENING KNIFE BLADES

4–23. Whether the blade's section is slender and parallel, or heavier and tapered, the sharpening action is similar. The bench stone may be a Japanese water stone, a diamond or ceramic hone, because our primary consideration at the moment is the geometry of the operation.

Laying the blade flat on the stone with the sharp edge pointing away, raise the back of the blade the required amount to incline the blade at the prescribed angle of approximately 5 degrees. Use whichever of the means is preferred to ascertain this as described above. Push the blade away, with pressure on the leading edge to be honed, trying to retain the angle and maintain consistently the area of bevel contact with the stone. The latter point is important to create a bevel and not a concave face. Such a condition would be detrimental since this would probably increase the angle at the cutting edge.

4–24. As the bevel increases in width on each side of the blade, control is necessary to produce a balanced, symmetrical edge.

Frequent examination of the bevel is recommended to ensure that the angular contact is being sustained. After a little careful practice, this comes with confidence and security.

When the edge is thought to be sharp or close to it, there is the need for some judgment of what is meant by sharp. A practical way to approach this is to hold the blade under a bright light and look along the edge, rocking the blade from side to side to try to reflect the light on any flat spot or flaw. Objectively, one is looking for a so-called "candle"; this is a bright reflection of the light source appearing as a spark or flash on the extreme edge of the blade. Ideally, there will be no spark reflected, in which case, a perfectly sharp edge has been achieved. A disciplined approach to this examination is essential. Naturally, for the incising of grounds for inlay work, the point requires especial attention.

SHARPENING BLADES FOR THE CHANNEL CUTTER

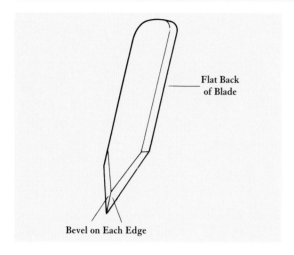

Flat Back
of Blade

Bevel on Each Edge

4–25. *Blades for the channel cutter have a bevel on only one side of the blade but on both edges. The bevels on both edges permits cutting in both directions along a periphery, while leaving one side of the cut perfectly square to the face of the ground.*

the type of blade and ways of sharpening, depending on the materials to be scraped and the results required.

Burnishing scraper blades calls for the use of a burnisher or "ticketer," the tool used to produce the characteristic burr that is, in effect, the scraper's cutting edge (**4–26**).

Consider first the plain cabinet scraper made from a rectangular piece of hardened spring steel. Its cutting edges may be "burred"

to give the scraper an effective cutting action. The burr may be coarse or fine, though in relative terms it is the nature of the scraper to produce a light cut to enhance the finished surface without tearing the wood fibers.

Processing from scratch with a new blade, we may consider the following sequence shown in **4–27** to **4–31**.

Illus. **4–32** to **4–39** show how to sharpen the blade for a two-handed scraper plane.

SHARPENING SCRAPER BLADES

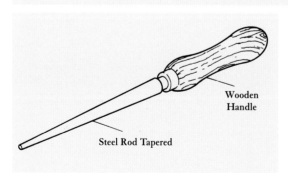

Wooden
Handle

Steel Rod Tapered

4–26. *The burnisher or "ticketer" is used to produce the characteristic burr that is, in effect, the scraper's cutting edge.*

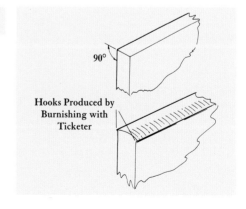

90°

Hooks Produced by
Burnishing with
Ticketer

4–27. *Top: Square, clean edges are essential features of the cabinet scraper, prior to burnishing. Bottom: The blade after burring the edges with the burnisher.*

SHARPENING SCRAPER BLADES (continued)

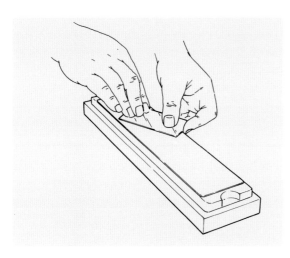

4–28. *"Flattening" the blade edge to remove old or redundant burrs. Any accidental blemishes should be removed from the face of the scraper by rubbing it across the surface of the stone.*

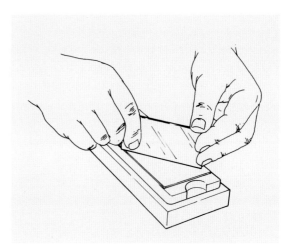

4–30. *The stroke is completed with the same orientation of the blade to the hone, but reversing the direction of travel. Repeating the forward and back strokes is continued, with frequent inspections, until the edge is clean, level, and square to the scraper blade face.*

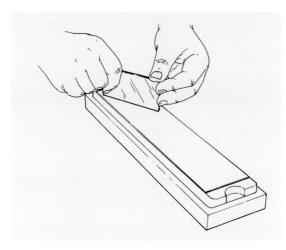

4–29. *Flatten and level the edge square to the face of the scraper. Setting the scraper blade at a diagonal during the traversing of the stone helps to keep the blade vertical while making the edge square with the sides of the blade. Commencing the push stroke with the blade held vertically, its edge is set at an angle across the hone. This helps to keep it upright as the blade is pushed along the hone.*

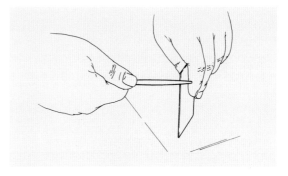

4–31. *Firm pressure is brought with the burnisher while stroking up and down, bearing the burnisher along the length of the blade edge. The object is to turn over the sharp corners to make the "hook," as shown here. Alternatively, the blade may be held in a vise for this purpose.*

SHARPENING ROUTER CUTTERS

By this is meant the blade from a hand router, otherwise called "old woman's tooth." Its cutter is essentially a shaft, whose sharpened edge is bent at a right angle and held by a special holder, incorporating a flat platform. The cutter projects through the base, cutting as the tool is brought into contact with the work surface.

Sharpening the cutter requires exactly the same technique as sharpening a beveled chisel **(4–40** to **4–42)**.

KNIFE APPLICATIONS

Before going further with an examination of the following methods, it is important to establish some terms of reference. In this book, the word "face" always refers to the exposed side, that is, the side that will become the viewable picture. "Back" always refers to the reverse side of the picture (the side against the wall). Whether working from the face or back, these terms will not vary.

Whichever knife is chosen for cutting out marquetry pieces, it is likely to be ground to make a bevel on each side of the blade to create a sharp edge. With the knife held vertically and drawn into the veneer, it creates a "V"-shaped groove. When the two parts are severed, it follows that the cut edge on each divided piece is at an angle off the vertical **(4–43)**. What has happened in physical terms is that the knife, as it is driven into the material, compresses the fibers on both sides of the cut, causing this distortion. It is also likely that some of the compression caused by this action may be recovered as the fibers of the wood absorb liquid glue that will be applied in the assembly process.

It is this beveled effect that gives rise to the need to decide which to use of four fundamental techniques, namely: vertical cutting from the face, vertical cutting from the back, bevel cutting from the face, and bevel cutting from the back. Also, it is a controversial topic that arises when marquetarians disagree with the principles. When applied with precision, any method can produce excellent work.

VERTICAL CUTTING FROM THE FACE

If all the pieces of the design were cut accurately from the face, the result could be acceptable, with the proviso that when assembled there would probably be a slight gap

SHARPENING BLADES FOR TWO-HANDED SCRAPER PLANES

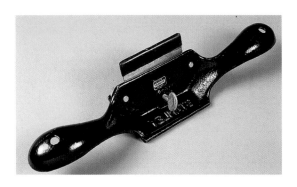

4–32. *A two-handed scraper plane, with a blade whose adjustment includes projection and the amount of "buckle" in the blade flexion. In the deflection of the blade lies the means of efficient operation of this tool. Without the slight buckling, the blade is too flexible, causing chattering and scarring of the wood surface.*

SHARPENING BLADES FOR TWO-HANDED SCRAPER PLANES (continued)

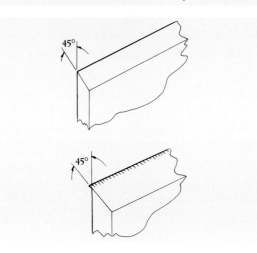

4–33. *Top: A blade from a scraper plane, or two-handed scraper. Unlike the cabinet scraper, its blade edge is somewhat chisel-like and ground at 45 degrees. Bottom: The sharp edge has been burred over with the burnisher.*

Remove the old burrs from the face as described in the preparation of the cabinet scraper and grind or file the edge at 45 degrees to the face. Lay the scraper flat on the bench with its bevel downward and "draw" the edge with the burnisher. This should actually increase the sharpness of the edge and remove any blemishes that might mar the flatness of the edge.

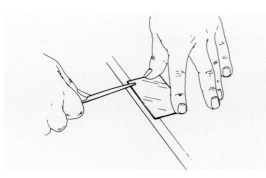

4–34. *Turn over the blade with bevel upward and proceed to stroke the edge. Make the stroke with the burnisher rubbing along on the bevel, burnishing it at 45 degrees to the face of the blade.*

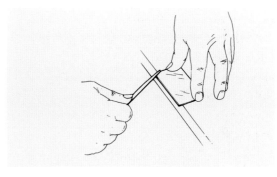

4–36. *The forward and back motion is continued, progressively lowering the angle of the burnisher.*

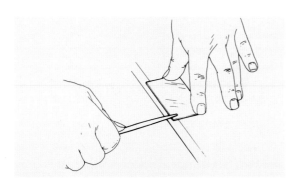

4–35. *Here the burnisher is shown having completed the first stroke.*

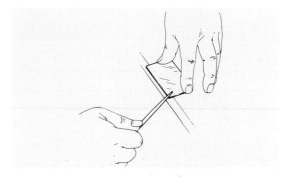

4–37. *The action continues, without undue pressure—just enough to coax the edge to turn over. Downward adjustment of the angle of the burnisher continues.*

SHARPENING BLADES FOR TWO-HANDED SCRAPER BLADES (continued)

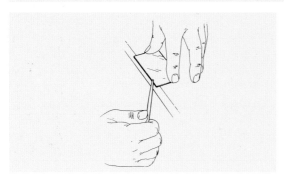

4–38. *Having burnished the edge a score of times or more, gradually the angle of burnisher is lowered until it is at a right angle to the tabletop, producing a burr in the process. This will produce a coarse burr that may be adjusted, by experiment, to give the desired cut. Remember, the idea is to get an extremely fine shaving from the surface of the work rather than fibrous dust.*

A hand-held cabinet scraper may be prepared in this way with a 45-degree edge if a coarse cut is needed.

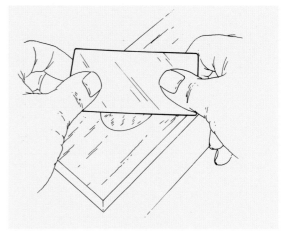

4–39. *Scraping with the sharpened scraper. Bowing the blade slightly, by pressing with the thumbs as the fingers restrain the edges, keeps the blade rigid during the scraping action.*

between the pieces. This is simply because of the angled sides left on each adjoining piece; the resulting join forms a "V." A liquid glue, such as PVA, will tend to swell the beveled fibers that were compressed by the knife, and this action will help to fill the spaces. Fortunately, when leveling with scraper and abrasive papers, if the face was cut from the front, this tends to reduce the gap between the pieces. However, there is a limit to how much of the veneer can be removed before reaching a point of hazardous thin-ness.

VERTICAL CUTTING FROM THE BACK

Almost everything said about the previous paragraph may be reversed in this description, except that if the design is to be seen as the original, it is necessary to reverse it for the cutting operation. Also, a disadvantage is found in leveling the face side in the finishing process, due to the widening of the gaps between the pieces, as more of the "V" is exposed.

BEVEL CUTTING FROM THE FACE

In this application, the knife is held at an angle to compensate for the bevel. The angle that presents the beveled edge, not the blade itself, is at 90 degrees to the surface. If this angle is maintained while using the edge of an aperture as a guide, it follows that the

Text Continues on Page 53

SHARPENING ROUTER CUTTERS

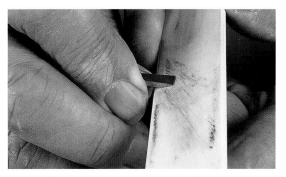

4–40. *Honing the bottom of the router cutter on a ceramic stone. Rubbing the cutter along the stone surface is intended to produce a sharp edge and remove any nicks or blemishes.*

4–41. *Following the sharpening of the bottom edge, the cutter is turned over and its top beveled edge is refined to remove any burrs created by the first action.*

4–42. *Once set up correctly, the hand router is a reliable tool and a great asset to the recessing operation.*

PROPER KNIFE-CUTTING POSITIONS

4–43. *Viewed from the front or back of the blade, when positioned for vertical cutting, the sides of the blade are at 90 degrees. The bevels on each side of the blade are at about 10 degrees from the vertical. Therefore, if it is required to make one side of the cut vertical, the blade would have to be inclined away from that side by 10 degrees.*

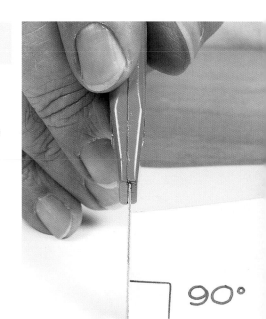

PROPER KNIFE-CUTTING POSITIONS (continued)

4–44. *Position 1. The knife is at its most vertical with the point in a piercing position; it is used for tiny apertures and negotiating very tight curves. Sometimes this position is applied in a direct stabbing action to pierce without any need to draw the blade along a line.*

4–45. *Position 2. Here the edge is just off the vertical, still in a partial stabbing mode but ready to be drawn along a line. It is used to start a cut in a sharp corner prior to following a connected line.*

4–46 *and* **4–47.** *Positions 3 and 4. These are the most common blade angles for normal application. They are neither too low, which would make penetration difficult, nor too high, which would impair continuity of line.*

4–48. *Position 5. More of the blade is in contact with the veneer in this position. This causes more drag, but at the same time, it helps to keep the blade in a straight line, guided by its own groove.*

CUTTING A LEAF-SHAPED APERTURE

4–49. *To commence the cut, Position 2 is applied, ensuring a clean entry into the sharp corner.*

4–50. *Position 4 is approached gradually without removing the blade. This is to keep control while following the smooth curve; the groove helps to hold the blade on course while allowing the required deviation.*

4–52. *See how the knife is turned toward the left, rotated by the finger and thumb.*

4–51. *Position 1 is applied by raising the knife gradually as the approach is made to the sharp corner. It may be necessary to reverse the blade point to pierce this corner cleanly, in the same manner as that for the commencement of the cut. The sequence would be repeated for the other, similar, side-to-finish cutting out of the leaf shape.*

Negotiating some tight bends or serpentine curves as certain designs require may be aided by twisting the knife during its traverse. Here the thumb and index fingers are used to create a rocking motion.

4–53. *Here the rotation of the knife is to the right (in contrast to the previous example) and is achieved by a reverse action of the index finger and thumb.*

CUTTING CURVED MOTIFS

4–54 *to* **4–57.** *For continuously curving motifs, the author uses a revolving work board, known as a "Lazy Susan." This is intended to be used to pass serving dishes around in the center of a dining table. As illustrated in the sequence, the cutting attitude of the hand holding the knife is maintained with little change, while the left hand rotates the work board. The green rectangle mounted on top of the Lazy Susan is the cutting mat.*

4–55.

4–56.

CUTTING CURVED MOTIFS (continued)

4–57.

piece to be inserted should make a close fit. Prior to cutting the piece to be inserted, it may be viewed through the aperture and positioned for optimum arrangement of grain distribution and color.

BEVEL CUTTING FROM THE BACK

If it is important to view the picture in its original form, a copy must be made in reverse. In many cases a picture, such as a landscape, may be reversed without noticeable errors, but a scene that contained, for instance, text, would be recognized immediately if it had been reversed. So, this must be considered at the composition stage.

The foregoing has dealt with the angles between the side of the blade and the work surface. In the cutting operation, there is another angle to consider, and that is the angle between the cutting edge and the work surface. In most cases, the knife blade will be pointed with a straight cutting edge. The angle it makes with the work surface is readily variable by raising or lowering the hand that is gripping the knife.

It is most normal to hold the knife as one holds a pen; most of the sideways control is achieved by pressure between the thumb and middle finger, with downward pressure given by the index finger bearing down. The other two fingers are used to support the hand and maintain its lateral positioning. Manipulation of the three digits holding the handle of the knife can raise or lower the knife's position, resulting in increasing or decreasing the angle between the cutting edge and the work surface.

CUTTING TECHNIQUES

An accepted system of cutting positions with a knife is numbered 1 to 5 as shown in **4–44** to **4–48**.

Illus. **4–49** to **4–53** show how a leaf-shaped aperture is negotiated using three of the positions described.

CUTTING CURVED MOTIFS

Illus. **4–54** to **4–57** depict how to cut continuously curving motifs using a Lazy Susan work board.

CHAPTER 5

MARQUETRY TECHNIQUES

In this chapter I discuss two methods of creating marquetry. One is a method in which the drawing is used as a "window." **(5–1** to **5–65)**. The second consists of stack- or pad-cutting with a scroll saw **(5–66** to **5–97)**. Finally, I offer some advice for mounting the finished marquetry **(5–98)**.

A "WINDOW" METHOD PROJECT

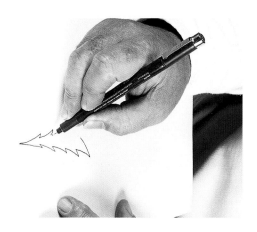

5–1. *For this demonstration (**5–1** to **5–65**), a simple drawing was made to represent a tree standing on a hillside. There are only five elements: a three-part tree on a background of hill and sky.*

An ink outline is drawn with a drafting pen of the type used by draftsmen. This pen produces a definite line, ideal for this purpose because it will show clearly through the film to be used later.

A "WINDOW" METHOD PROJECT (continued)

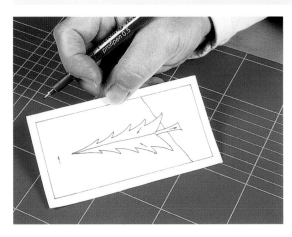

5–2. *A border is added, using a rule, to complete the picture and the paper is trimmed to size. When the marquetry picture is finished, the area outside the borders will be removed to leave a clean edge. To assist in the selection of suitable veneers, small arrows are added to show, if necessary, the direction of the grain in the wood.*

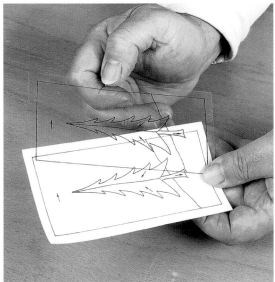

5–3. *A faithful copy is traced in ink on a piece of transparent film, cut to the same size as the paper. An alternative to transparent film is tracing paper, but due to the superior surface and durable nature of the film, it is preferable. Most art material suppliers should stock transparent film, possible called tracing or drafting film. For this example, it is assumed that the original design was intended to be viewed as drawn—that is, the drawing will be seen from the "front." This method requires the cutting to be done from the "back" of the work, so the design will be traced in reverse. In this particular design, it is not necessary to reverse the tracing because no indication of left or right is discernible. But in some cases it might be important to replicate the original picture and then reverse the copy.*

5–4. *Veneer is chosen to represent the sky. It has a pale color and little grain pattern, to allow the darker form of the tree and hill to stand out in contrast. The veneer is cut to the same size as the film with the tracing; it will also form the base layer of the marquetry picture. The film is attached to the top edge of the veneer base.*

A "WINDOW" METHOD PROJECT (continued)

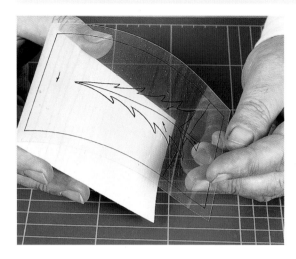

5–5. *With transparent adhesive tape correctly attached, the film and base veneer are joined by the "hinge." When required, the tracing may be overlaid on the base to view the work as it progresses.*

5–6. *Between the tracing and the base veneer, a sheet of carbon paper is placed with the shiny side down, and the whole drawing is traced. A conventional ballpoint pen that has run out of ink is used for this, because it is better not to apply any more ink to the tracing. Care must be taken because these transferred lines will become the cutting guide for the individual elements in the picture.*

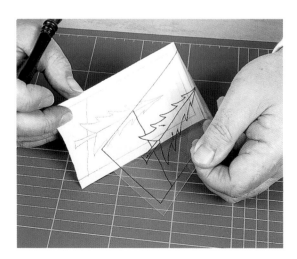

5–7. *The picture has been correctly transferred to the base veneer from the film tracing.*

A "WINDOW" METHOD PROJECT (continued)

5–8. *Application of the first cut is made along the line dividing the sky from the hill. This first cut is just enough to sever the surface fibers of the veneer, hardly more than tracing the outline of the hilltop. It is at this point that consideration is given to the angle of the side of the blade. The edge of the cut must be as vertical as possible in order to make a matching joint with the adjacent portion. In order to achieve this, the blade is held so it leans away from the finished cut, allowing its beveled edge to produce a vertical cut.*

The cut is made through the border areas, while also allowing the complete removal of the lower part of the design.

5–9. *A second cut is made, following the slight groove made by the first cut. Only the slightest pressure is applied to ensure a clean cut and to avoid the risk of splitting the wood.*

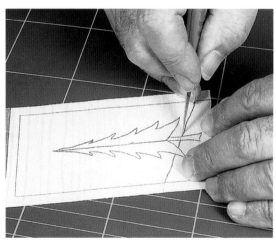

5–10. *This process is repeated until the two parts are separated. Gradually, experience will be gained which will enable the marquetarian to feel the pressure required to cut efficiently and to judge how many repeated cuts are needed. The hardness of the wood and its grain direction will determine this.*

A "WINDOW" METHOD PROJECT (continued)

5–11. *Veneer is chosen to represent the hill; it is placed beneath the sky/base veneer with its grain oriented to follow the slope of the horizon. The portion of the hill veneer is clearly seen through the transparent tracing.*

5–12. *After a satisfactory alignment of the hill veneer with the sky/base, the pieces are turned over and connected temporarily with adhesive tape. A low-tack type is used to allow removal without risk of damage to the materials.*

5–13. *When the two veneers are fixed together, the assembly is turned over and the transparent tracing is placed over the assembly. Carbon paper is put between the film and the veneers enabling a tracing to be made of the details of the borders that surround the hill portion. It is not necessary to trace the division between the hilltop and the sky because the sky will form a guide for the knife.*

A "WINDOW" METHOD PROJECT

5–14. *At the division between the sky and the hill, the knife is applied following the method described for cutting the lower edge of the sky. An advantage here is that the sky at the horizon will act as a guide for the knife. Similar caution is advised, observing the need to ease the knife gradually into the fibers of the veneer while making several light strokes to sever the material completely. The outside edges are also cut to separate the hill portion from the veneer sheet.*

5–15. *To be sure of severing all the fibers and avoiding any chance of splitting the veneer, extra pieces of tape are added as a support beneath the lower edge of the design and the horizon cut.*

5–16. *Finally the sky and the hill are separated cleanly.*

A "WINDOW" METHOD PROJECT (continued)

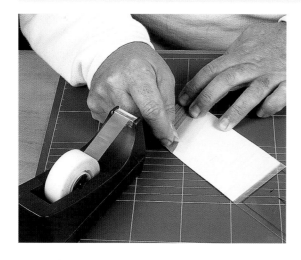

5–17. *Adhesive tape is applied to the back of the design to connect and retain, temporarily, the two veneer portions.*

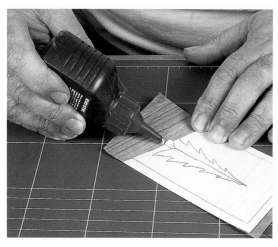

5–18. *A few drops of white PVA glue are applied to the front of the design where the two portions meet.*

5–19. *Using a fingertip, the glue is spread along and eased into the joint between the portions. The assembly is set aside to dry. PVA glue is easily removed from fingers if cleansed immediately. A damp cloth is sufficient and convenient for the workplace.*

A "WINDOW" METHOD PROJECT (continued)

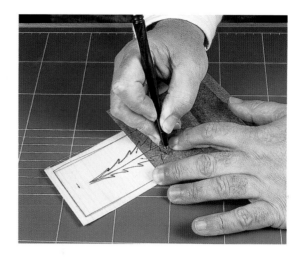

5–20. *With the two main parts of the design joined, they may be treated as one piece and the process can continue with the next stage. Having lost the design that was drawn on the lower part of the sky/base, it is necessary to replace the details on the hill portion. Once more the transparency is brought into place and a carbon copy of the lower part of the tree is traced onto the hill portion.*

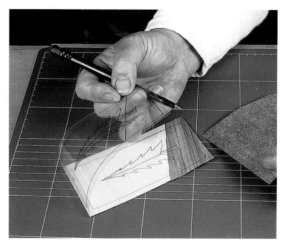

5–21. *There should now be an outline of the complete tree drawn in carbon on the combined portions that make up the base veneer.*

5–22. *Before commencing to cut out the apertures for the tree, some consideration should be given to the procedure. There are three elements making up the tree: left-hand branches, right-hand branches, and the trunk. They all contain outward-pointing V shapes. When cutting a V-shaped opening, it is generally better to cut from the point outward, in two cuts, rather than cut in toward the point of the V. This is to ensure a crisp, clean point that is easy to produce with a sharp-pointed knife. A degree of downward stabbing action is required at the start of the stroke to ensure the effectiveness of the cutting action. It is emphasized again that several light strokes are the best way.*

A "WINDOW" METHOD PROJECT (continued)

5–23. *When the complete outline of the left-hand branches has been cut, the section may be removed by stabbing it gently with the knife and lifting it out. If the cutting has been accomplished correctly, this will be an uneventful operation.*

5–24. *Using the aperture made by the removal of the left-hand branches as a "window," the veneer chosen for the branches may be viewed. As a silhouette against the light sky, the tree color would be somewhat dark, so a brown shade is suggested. Bearing in mind that there would be a tendency for the branches on such a tree to be angled downward, grain direction is an important consideration.*

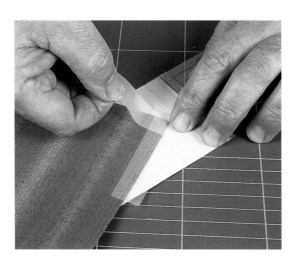

5–25. *When a satisfactory portion of the veneer chosen for the branches is orientated for the best effect, low-tack tape is placed on the back of the design to temporarily hold it in place. Tape is used to cover the piece to support the edges during the cutting process, to help protect from accidental splitting.*

A "Window" Method Project (continued)

5–26. *A slender, sharply pointed knife is used for this work as the aperture is used as a guide; a close fit is required. Light stabbing cuts are needed to obtain clean points in the V shape, and as was done in the cutting of the branch aperture, working away from the points is better.*

5–27. *A practical tip for checking on the status of a cutting operation is to hold up to the light the portion being cut. The light shows through the cut revealing any areas not severed completely. It is then a straightforward matter to refine the cut to perfection.*

5–28. *Having removed the left-hand branch section from the veneer sheet, it is placed in the aperture and checked for fit. If there is any discrepancy, it is possible at this stage to create another piece with, hopefully, more success. This is an advantage not available to many other crafts and it is one that should be used wherever necessary. There is the prospect of the wood expanding very slightly when adhesive is absorbed into the grain during the gluing process, but this is best seen as a bonus to tighten up the almost perfect fit, rather than as a cure for a bad joint. When a satisfactory fit is achieved, the branch is inserted into its aperture and retained with low-tack tape.*

A "WINDOW" METHOD PROJECT (continued)

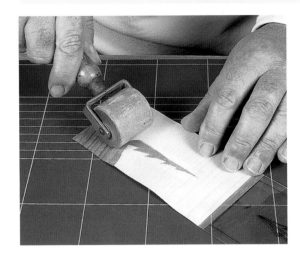

5–29. *To ensure the pieces are level and flat, a roller is applied firmly across the surface of the assembly. A common roller used to press wallpaper edges is fine for this purpose.*

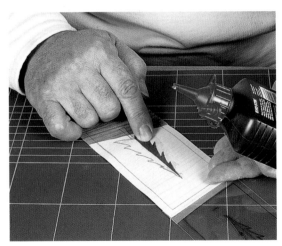

5–30. *Adhesive is pressed into the joint between the branch and its aperture, but leaving out glue from the straight joint that runs down the center of the tree. This is simply because the right-hand branch is next to be cut out and the center joint will be used as one of the cutting guides.*

5–31. *A method similar to that used for the left-hand branches is applied to cutting out the aperture for the right-hand branches. As mentioned above, there is no need to cut down the centerline of the tree, since it was already cut in the previous operation.*

A "WINDOW" METHOD PROJECT (continued)

5–32. *Few problems should arise from cutting out this portion. Remember, as always, to lean the blade away from the edge of the aperture to leave the side vertical.*

5–33. *Position beneath the aperture the same veneer sheet from which was cut the left-hand branches. Arrange the grain to follow the same descending angle as the right-hand branches to make a mirror image with the left-hand section. It may well appear to be of slightly different shades, but this is due to the lay of the wood fibers reflecting light at different angles. It also enhances the effect of the two halves.*

5–34. *As before, the design is reversed and low-tack tape is applied to hold in position the veneer to be cut. It is worth bearing in mind that the tape helps to reinforce the edges during the cutting process, so no corners should be untaped.*

A "WINDOW" METHOD PROJECT (continued)

5–35. *Proceed as with the cutting of the first branches.*

5–36. *Remove the branch section when severed completely and replace it to check for accurate fitting. If all is well, tape it in position within the aperture.*

5–37. *Glue is rubbed in to secure the piece.*

A "WINDOW" METHOD PROJECT (continued)

5–38. *As the remaining aperture is for the tree trunk, this crosses from the top to the bottom of the design, connecting the bottom of the sky to the top of the hill. No special instructions are necessary except that, as always, it is important to be mindful of working from corners rather than into them.*

5–39. *Tape and glue hold together the sky and hill parts, so that the section cut out for the trunk will come away in one piece, as shown in the illustration.*

5–40. *A darker colored wood is used for the trunk, as would be the case in nature. This is viewed through the aperture, as usual, to help decide which part of the veneer to use.*

A "WINDOW" METHOD PROJECT (continued)

5–41. *Selected for its dark, stripey appearance, the veneer suitable for the trunk is hard and brittle. To obviate difficulties in cutting through the aperture, after marking the outline lightly with the point of the knife, the veneer is removed.*

5–42. *To help cut this obstinate wood, lightly dampen it with a wet cloth prior to deepening the cut.*

5–43. *Tape is added to the underside of the piece to support the edges in the hope of preventing splintering.*

A "WINDOW" METHOD PROJECT (continued)

5–44. *A sharply honed blade, applied discretely, is, as always, the answer. Using the point of the knife, the trunk is removed cleanly from its aperture.*

5–45. *Low-tack tape is applied to the back of the design to hold the trunk in place.*

5–46. *A small dab of adhesive is applied and rubbed in with the fingertip.*

A "WINDOW" METHOD PROJECT (continued)

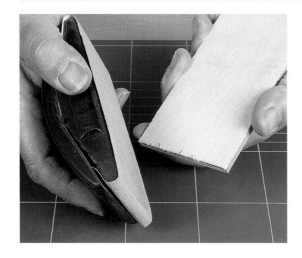

5–47. *Plywood, cut approximately to the size of the design, is prepared for the backing board. Its surface is rubbed down to level and cleaned using an abrasive paper and a rubbing block.*

5–48. *Edges are given special treatment to ensure that nothing protrudes to prevent the design from lying flat.*

5–49. *To make sure that everything is in place, the completed marquetry panel is viewed through the transparent film for the last time. Provided all is correct, the film is removed and set aside until such time that it might be used again.*

A "WINDOW" METHOD PROJECT (continued)

5–50. *One last inspection to make sure that the marquetry panel and the backing board are similar in size.*

5–51. *A very coarse abrasive paper is attached to the rubbing block.*

5–52. *With a scrubbing action, the coarse abrasive is applied to roughen the surface of the plywood backing on the face to receive the adhesive. This will produce a better surface to which the glue will adhere, and consequently, will affix more securely to the marquetry panel.*

A "WINDOW" METHOD PROJECT (continued)

5–53. *Using a glue brush, apply a coat of PVA adhesive to the roughened face of the backing board. Imagine it to be paint and apply a proper volume of glue to cover the whole surface.*

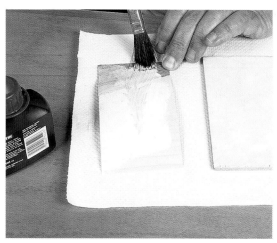

5–54. *Apply a light coat of the PVA adhesive to the back of the marquetry panel, making sure that there are no dry spots. When the panel is covered, there will be a tendency for it to curve upward as the wood absorbs the glue.*

5–55. *Bring the panel and the backing board together with care to see that no air is trapped between the two glued faces. This can be managed well enough if working from one end in a rocking motion.*

A "WINDOW" METHOD PROJECT (continued)

5–56. *Cover the panel with a piece of clean cardboard of the same size.*

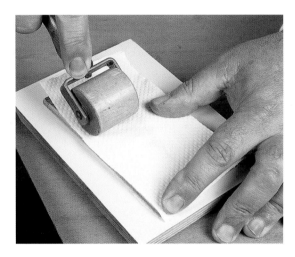

5–57. *Use the roller fastidiously to press together the panel and the backing. Excess adhesive will probably squeeze out from between the layers, but this is to be expected. It can be cleaned off with a damp cloth.*

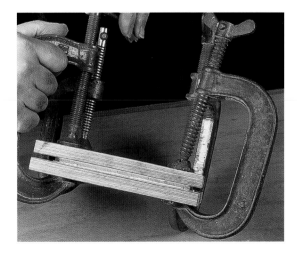

5–58. *Two pieces of plastic-faced clamping boards are used, one on either side of the glued layers. Plastic-facing prevents any escaping glue from adhering to the clamping boards. If plastic-faced boards are not available, use plain boards and place a tissue next to the panel layers to protect them from glue. A clamp at each corner ensures overall pressure during the setting of the glue.*

A "WINDOW" METHOD PROJECT (continued)

5–59. *After 24 hours, to be sure of the curing of the adhesive, the clamps are removed and the panel inspected. A knife is used to score the borders of the panel in preparation for sawing the edges.*

5–60. *Rest the marquetry picture on the work surface and hold it firmly. If your hands are not strong enough, use a clamp to secure the picture while the borders are sawn away.*

5–61. *With fine abrasive paper attached to the rubbing block, the marks left by the saw are smoothed away to leave clean sides with no imperfections.*

A "WINDOW" METHOD PROJECT (continued)

5–62. *When the sides are smoothed, the front of the picture should be rubbed with the abrasive paper. Use gentle but thorough strokes to remove any roughness. Apply just enough pressure to clean away any imperfections and level the surface.*

5–63. *A sealing coat of varnish is applied to the picture; when absolutely dry, it is rubbed with fine abrasive paper. Repeat the varnishing and rubbing down several times until the whole surface has an even, clear, and smooth surface.*

5–64. *A final treatment is to apply, with a pad of wire wool, a coat of wax polish to the surface. This imparts a silky finish of great depth and quality.*

A "WINDOW" METHOD PROJECT (continued)

5–65. *The completed picture is ready for display.*

STACK-CUTTING METHOD USING A SCROLL SAW

A popular alternative to knife-cut marquetry is a method that uses a scroll saw (a powered fretsaw). This method is more common in the United States than elsewhere, probably due to its suitability for cutting the thicker veneers that are produced by sawing rather than peeling wood from the log.

Another advantage is that sawing overcomes the problems of cutting hard woods and difficult grain configurations that may be impossible with a knife.

By arranging the different parts of a drawing to be cut from different sheets that are then stacked together to form a pad, it is possible to cut all the parts at once.

A simple design has been chosen to demonstrate the method, in the following step-by-step project (**5–66** to **5–97**).

STACK-CUTTING WITH A SCROLL SAW

5–66. *Choose a subject, either an original picture or an existing design. In the example shown, the design is from a famous painting by Vincent van Gogh.*

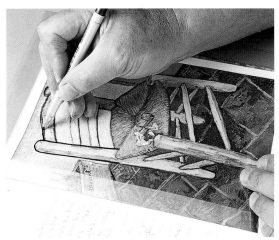

5–67. *A sheet of film is laid over the original design and traced over to produce a "transparency."*

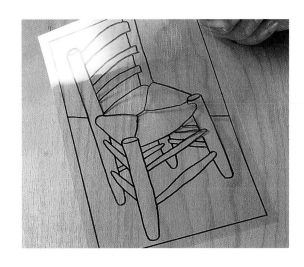

5–68. *A margin of about ½ inch (12 mm) is allowed all around the picture. Any amendments to the original, such as details to be ignored, are made on the transparency. For example, the separate floor tiles are left out and so are the objects that were resting on the chair.*

STACK-CUTTING WITH A SCROLL SAW (continued)

5–69. *Using the transparency, a copy is made, either by a conventional office photocopier or by a computer scanner. Marks are made at each corner to enable realignment of the transparency and the copy.*

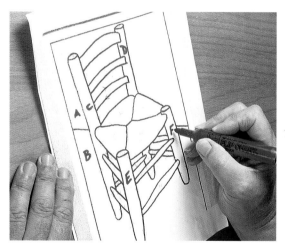

5–70. *Arrows are marked to show the desirable grain direction on each element.*

5–71. *Cardboard, rather than veneer, is used for the layers to be wasted. The cardboard is equal in thickness to the veneer. Six layers are cut to the same size as the transparency and all are marked at the corners with registration marks to ensure correct alignment.*

STACK-CUTTING WITH A SCROLL SAW (continued)

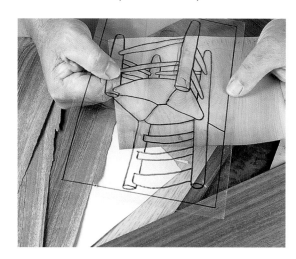

5–72. *Specimens of veneer are aligned beneath each element of the picture outlined in the transparency and are considered in terms of color and grain pattern to suit the original picture. The chair seat, for instance, has four parts, each requiring a different grain direction and, if possible, it should suggest a curved edge of a seat made from rush (a coarse grass used for seating or baskets). This is a straightforward process due to the simple, direct manner of the brushwork, of which van Gogh was a master.*

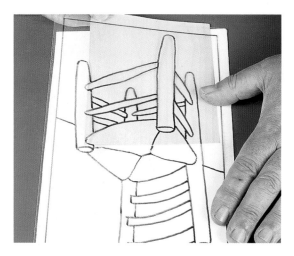

5–73. *Beginning with the chair legs, the chosen veneer is placed between the waste cardboard and the transparency, beneath a chair leg.*

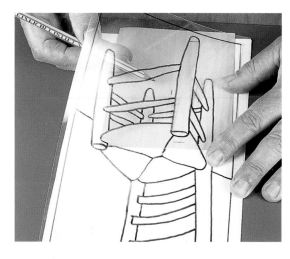

5–74. *Raising the transparency, four marks are made on the veneer: one on each side to represent the width of the leg, and one at the top and bottom for the height. The marks are made purely by eye and a little extra is added all around, say, up to ¼ inch (6 mm), allowing for a margin of error.*

STACK-CUTTING WITH A SCROLL SAW (continued)

5–75. *Using the four marks as a guide, a rectangle is drawn on the veneer with pencil and rule.*

5–76. *With the marquetry knife, the rectangle marked on the veneer is cut out cleanly.*

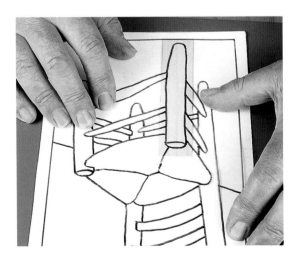

5–77. *To check that the veneer rectangle is the correct size, once more it is placed beneath the outline of the chair leg.*

STACK-CUTTING WITH A SCROLL SAW (continued)

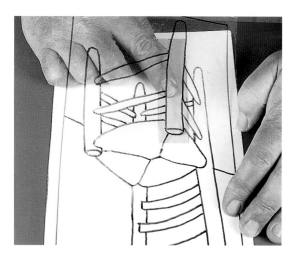

5–78. *If all is well, the first waste layer is placed beneath the transparency with the corner register marks aligned. The veneer rectangle is placed on the waste layer, beneath the outline of the chair leg, where it is held with a fingertip.*

5–79. *The veneer rectangle is retained while the transparency is set aside. Using a pencil, the outline of the rectangle is marked on the waste layer.*

5–80. *With a straightedge as a guide, the rectangle marked on the waste layer is cut out, leaving the pencil mark, to ensure a close fit of the veneer rectangle.*

Stack-Cutting with a Scroll Saw (continued)

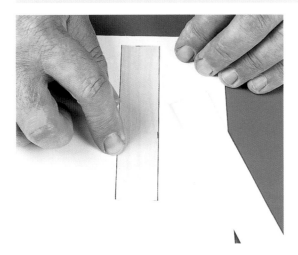

5–81. *When the rectangle has been lifted from the waste layer, it is replaced with the veneer rectangle. If some trimming is necessary to ensure a good fit, this is the time to do it. However, it is not necessary to make a perfect marriage, as long as the two parts fit reasonably well.*

5–82. *Adhesive tape is applied to retain the veneer in the waste layer.*

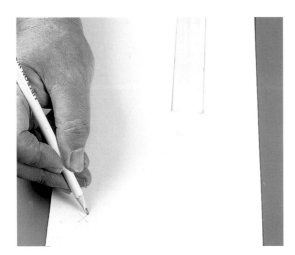

5–83. *A cross is marked in the top left-hand corner to show the orientation of the sheet. This will be a practical aid when the sorting of the layers takes place.*

STACK-CUTTING WITH A SCROLL SAW (continued)

5–84. *The same process is repeated, as described in **5–7** to **5–17**, for all the other elements in the picture. Some of the layers may contain several elements for convenience—bearing in mind the subsequent sawing process, the fewer the layers, the better.*

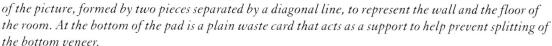

Above, the layers are shown in a fan, prior to arranging them in a stack to form the marquetry pad. Registration marks and the orientation crosses should be aligned accurately in each layer.

On top of the pad is the copy with the outlined picture. The lowest veneer layer is the background of the picture, formed by two pieces separated by a diagonal line, to represent the wall and the floor of the room. At the bottom of the pad is a plain waste card that acts as a support to help prevent splitting of the bottom veneer.

5–85. *When all the layers are arranged correctly they are stacked, in readiness for the sawing oper-ation, by pinning them together with veneer pins or other fine nails. It is best to use a length of pin appropriate to the thickness of the pad, that is, long enough to penetrate all layers, but not so long as to extend too far out from the pad. Small pins are best positioned with tweezers, as shown, for the nailing operation.*

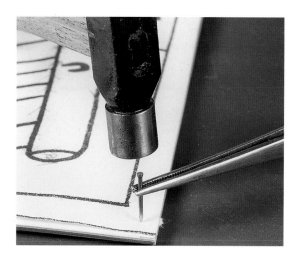

5–86. *It will be necessary to drill some small holes in the design to admit the saw blade, because there are apertures to be cut without access from the side of the picture. For this, a small drill holder is used, easily operated with one hand while the other hand holds the pad.*

STACK-CUTTING WITH A SCROLL SAW (continued)

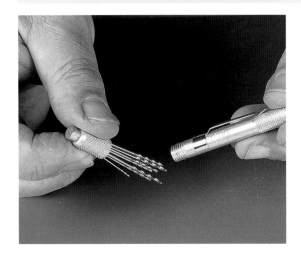

5–87. *Several types of drill holder are available; this one has a hollow body to house the drill bits. A magnetic cap retains the tiny drill bits, and allows easy management of their selection, removal and return when the drilling operation is completed.*

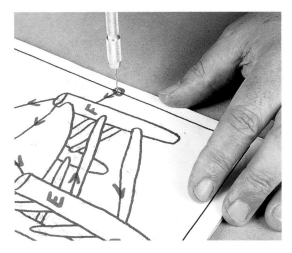

5–88. *Location of the access holes will depend to a large extent on the type of design. A corner, or a change of line direction, is useful and the entry hole may be unnoticed when the sawing is done and the pieces are assembled. It may also be noted, that, where lines interconnect, the saw may change direction to incorporate several elements in a continuous line of sawing. This requires planning and may be shown by marking with arrows the entry points of the saw blade and the direction of sawing.*

5–89. *Many makes of scroll saw are available; this is a heavy-duty model, with a large capacity and a wide range of applications. Even the least expensive and most basic scroll saw will suffice and they all are capable of sawing a marquetry pad.*

STACK-CUTTING WITH A SCROLL SAW (continued)

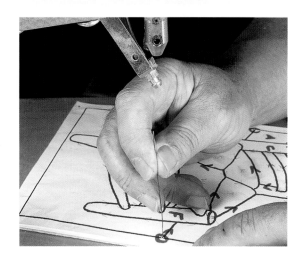

5–90. *For entering the saw blade in the first hole, a fine blade is advisable to make a good joint between the elements; but for photographic purposes, a coarse one was used for the demonstration shown here.*

5–91. *A sophisticated accessory is fitted to the Diamond scroll saw, incorporating a hold-down foot to prevent the work from rising during the sawing. Behind the blade is a buffer to prevent excessive deflection of the blade rearward and a bar is adjusted to protect one's fingers from accidentally touching the moving blade.*

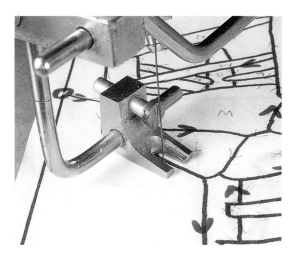

5–92. *Sawing progresses along the outlines following the prescribed arrows, reminiscent of the puzzle mazes found in children's books.*

STACK-CUTTING WITH A SCROLL SAW (continued)

5–93. *A board of waste veneer is used as a backing to support the layer of cutout elements. Having removed the pieces, one layer at a time, careful identification is made and each one is subjected to a trial fit.*

5–94. *Each piece of the design is glued into its correct position and finally clamped, to dry completely.*

5–95. *All the pieces are fitted and glued. The picture now looks like a jigsaw puzzle, but differing from the norm, because many more pieces will be discarded than will be used.*

STACK-CUTTING WITH A SCROLL SAW (continued)

5–96. *When the glue is completely dry, the surface of the marquetry is leveled with a scraper, finished with a fine abrasive paper, and coated in an oil finish. (See Appendix for finishing techniques.)*

5–97. *The relatively coarse blade leaves gaps between the pieces. These are filled with patent wood filler, of dark color, emphasizing the outlines of the objects in the picture, much as the artist did in his painting.*

MOUNTING THE WORK

Mounting a piece of marquetry on a rigid backing board not only protects its inherent fragility but also provides a means by which it may be framed or displayed. Marquetry pictures may be fixed by an adhesive to a variety of grounds, such as man-made particleboards or plywood. See Adhesives on pages 37 and 38.

If the piece is to be framed, in the normal way of framing a painting or photograph, a relatively thin board will be satisfactory for the backing, say 3/16 inch (4 mm) thick. Most marquetry pictures are presented without a frame, but with the edges covered with a veneer. Sometimes a border is added by inlaying lines. Other pictures are bordered with a veneer to give the illusion of a solid separate frame. Several examples are shown in the examples on pages 101 to 105.

The author's preference is to mount the work on a rigid board, but for those who prefer to add a separate frame, the same principles apply as to the framing of any other picture, and this subject is dealt with substantially on the following pages.

Whichever is decided upon, it is necessary to back the board on the opposite side to the picture with a waste veneer to "balance" the assembly. If a balancer is not added to the back of the picture, severe warping will almost certainly occur in time, and this will ruin the desirable flat surface.

If a border is to be added **(5–98)**, reference to **5–99** to **5–105** showing various ways of inlaying should provide inspiration and information to achieve this.

MOUNTING THE WORK

5–98. *"Quiet Byways," by Janet McBain, is a fine example of a simple but effective line border to frame her beautiful marquetry picture.*

MOUNTING THE WORK (continued)

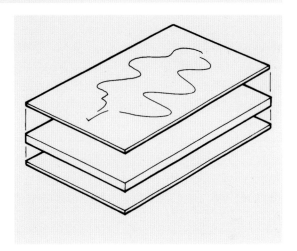

5–99. *A layered stack of three elements is made using the completed marquetry picture, a mounting board, and a backing board. The mounting board may be a piece of plywood, blockboard, or medium-density fiberboard, and the backing board is made from a piece of veneer of similar thickness to that used in the marquetry picture.*

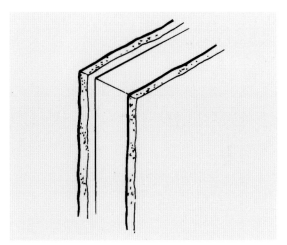

5–100. *Slight overlapping of the two outer layers is allowed for, in order that they may be trimmed level after the three-layer stack is glued. Clamping is similar to the application described in mounting the completed marquetry picture that used the window method.*

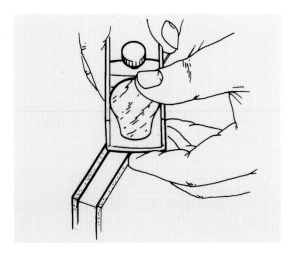

5–101. *When the glue has dried completely, using a sharp plane, the edges of all three layers in the stack are trimmed level and smooth.*

MOUNTING THE WORK (continued)

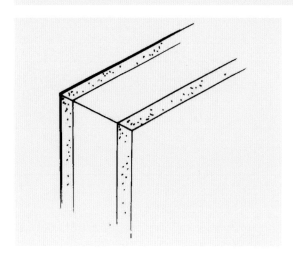

5–102. *All sides must be straight and square to the faces of the stack in preparation for the application of the borders.*

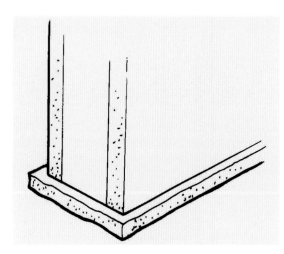

5–103. *Veneer selected for the border is cut into strips a little wider than the thickness of the stack, as shown. It is best to use an impact adhesive for this application. The normal application of impact adhesives is as follows: apply the adhesive to each part to be glued and allow each part to become dry to the touch. Bring the parts together, making sure that they are aligned correctly, and the firm pressure ensures an instant adhesion.*

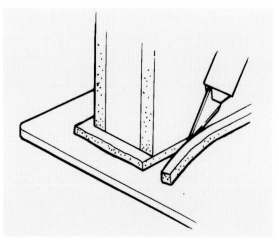

5–104. *Excess veneer is trimmed away with a knife. Keep the edge firmly resting on the cutting mat for this purpose. Treat all four edges in the same way.*

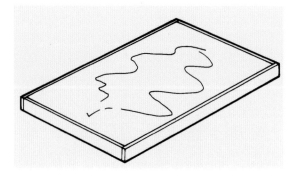

5–105. *Because the borders are made from thin veneer, it is not necessary to miter the corners. A gentle rub down with a light abrasive is all that is necessary to finish the border.*

CHAPTER 6

VENEER EXAMPLES

It's helpful to have an idea of the range of veneer colors available. This chapter presents a range of commonly available veneers.

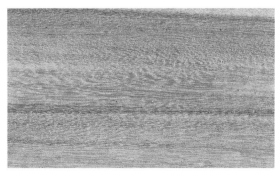

ABOVE **6–1.** *Afara* (Terminalia superba)
TOP RIGHT: **6–2.** *Afrormosia* (Afrormosia elata)
BOTTOM RIGHT: **6–3.** *Agba* (Nigerian cedar)
(Gossweilerodendron balsamiferum)

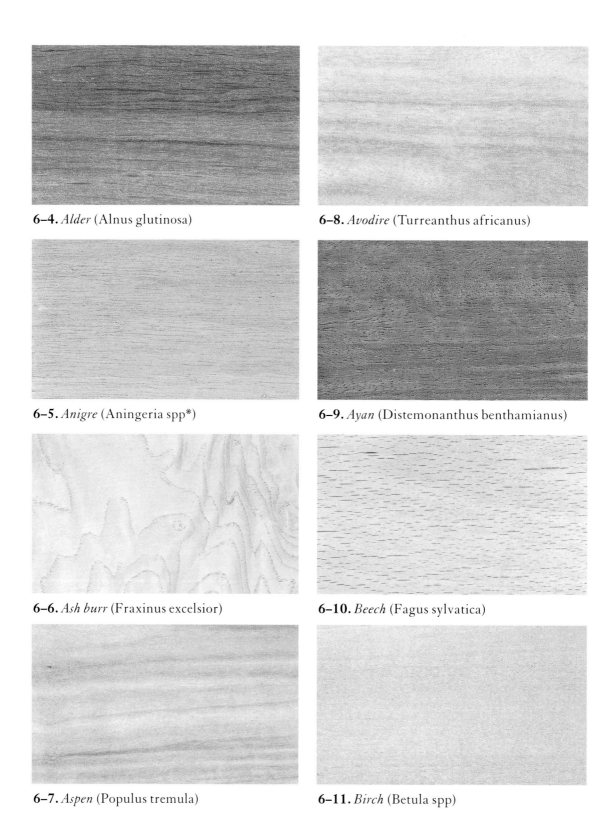

6–4. *Alder* (Alnus glutinosa)

6–8. *Avodire* (Turreanthus africanus)

6–5. *Anigre* (Aningeria spp*)

6–9. *Ayan* (Distemonanthus benthamianus)

6–6. *Ash burr* (Fraxinus excelsior)

6–10. *Beech* (Fagus sylvatica)

6–7. *Aspen* (Populus tremula)

6–11. *Birch* (Betula spp)

*spp refers to species

6–12. *Bubinga* (Guibortia spp)

6–16. *Chestnut (horse)* (Aesculus hippocastanum)

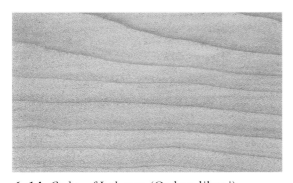

6–13. *Castello*

6–17. *Chestnut (sweet)* (Castanea sativa)

6–14. *Cedar of Lebanon* (Cedrus libani)

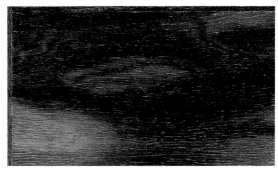

6–18. *Ebony, macassar* (Diospyros celebica)

6–15. *Cherry* (Prunus avium)

6–19. *Elm* (Ulmus procera)

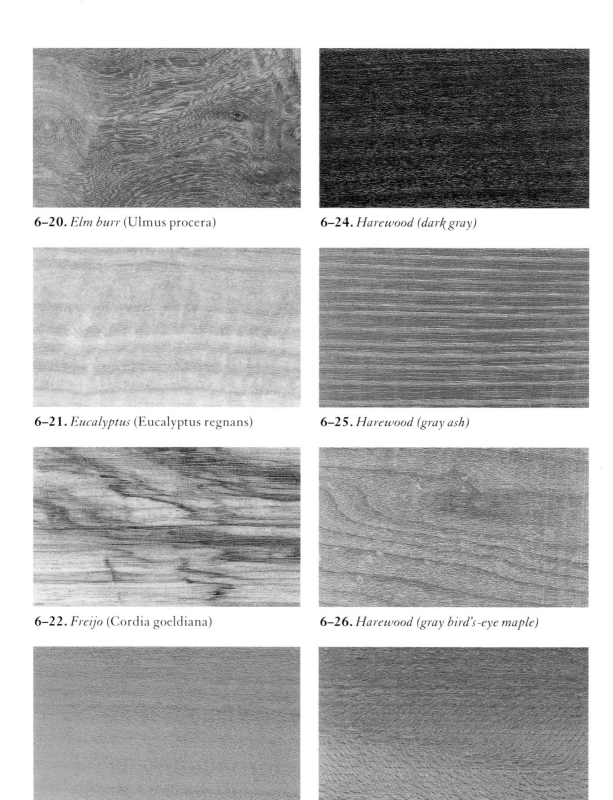

6–20. *Elm burr* (Ulmus procera)

6–24. *Harewood (dark gray)*

6–21. *Eucalyptus* (Eucalyptus regnans)

6–25. *Harewood (gray ash)*

6–22. *Freijo* (Cordia goeldiana)

6–26. *Harewood (gray bird's-eye maple)*

6–23. *Harewood (blue)*

6–27. *Harewood (gray plane)*

6–28. *Harewood (mid-gray)*

6–32. *Iroko* (Chlorophora excelsa)

6–29. *Harewood (silver-gray Indian)*

6–33. *Koto* (Pterygota spp)

6–30. *Hornbeam* (Carpinus betulus)

6–34. *Larch* (Larix europa)

6–31. *Imboia* (Phoebe porosa)

6–35. *Laurel, Indian* (Terminaria elata)

6–36. *Lime (basswood in United States)* (Tilia vulgaris)

6–40. *Makore* (Mimusops heckelii)

6–37. *Magnolia* (Magnolia spp)

6–41. *Mansonia* (Mansonia altissima)

6–38. *Mahogany, Brazilian* (Swietenia macrophylla)

6–42. *Maple (bird's-eye)* (Acer saccharum)

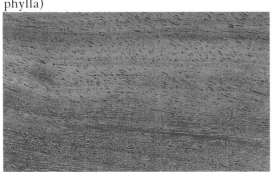

6–39. *Mahogany curl* (Swietenia macrophylla)

6–43. *Maple burr* (Acer saccharum)

6–44. *Myrtle burr* (Umbellularia californica)

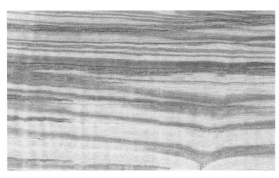

6–48. *Olive ash* (Fraxinus excelsior)

6–45. *Oak, brown* (Quercus robur)

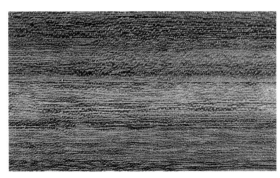

6–49. *Olive, tropical* (Olea hochstetteri)

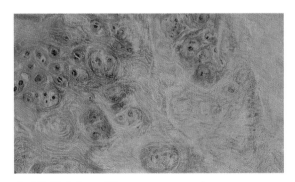

6–46. *Oak burr* (Quercus petraea)

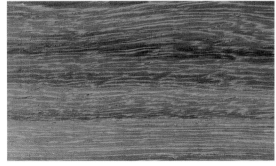

6–50. *Padauk* (Ptreocarpus dalbergiodes)

6–47. *Oak, English* (Quercus petraea)

6–51. *Paldao* (Dracontomelum dao)

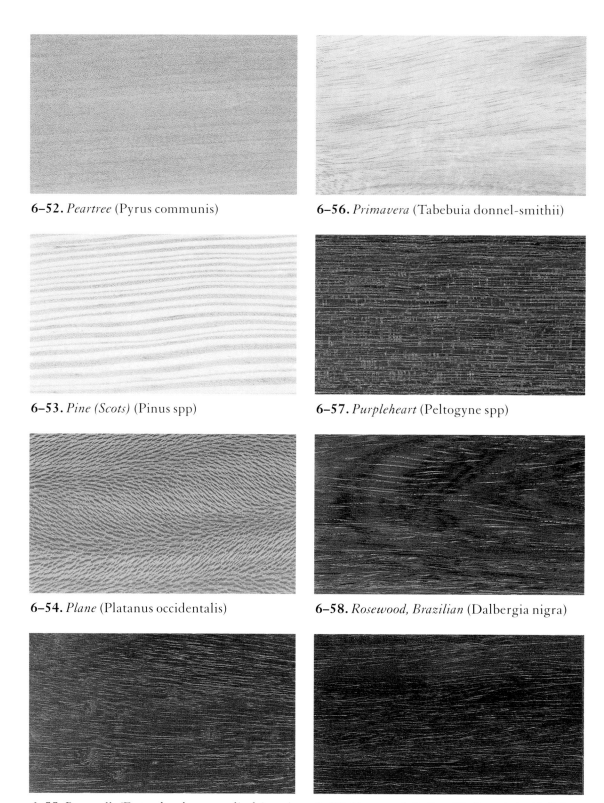

6–52. *Peartree* (Pyrus communis)

6–56. *Primavera* (Tabebuia donnel-smithii)

6–53. *Pine (Scots)* (Pinus spp)

6–57. *Purpleheart* (Peltogyne spp)

6–54. *Plane* (Platanus occidentalis)

6–58. *Rosewood, Brazilian* (Dalbergia nigra)

6–55. *Pommelle* (Entendrophagma cylindricum)

6–59. *Rosewood, Indian* (Dalbergia latifolia)

6–60. *Rosewood, San Domingo*

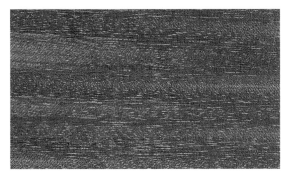

6–61. *Rosewood, Santos*

6–62. *Sapele* (Entandrophragma cylindricum)

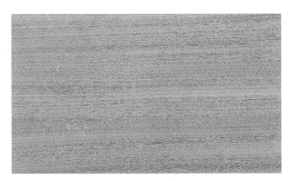

6–63. *Satinwood* (Chloroxylon swietania)

6–64. *Sycamore (Maple in the United States)* (Acer pseudoplatanus)

6–65. *Silky oak (Australian)* (Cardwellia sublimis)

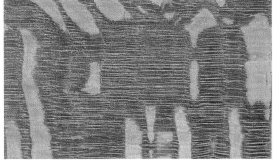

6–66. *Teak* (Tectona grandis)

6–67. *Walnut, African* (Lovoa klaneana)

6–68. *Walnut, American black* (Juglans nigra)

6–72. *Walnut, European* (Juglans regia)

6–69. *Walnut, Queensland* (Endiandra palmer-stonii)

6–73. *Wenge* (Millettia laurentil)

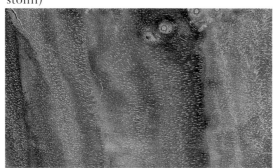

6–70. *Walnut burr, United States* (Juglans nigra)

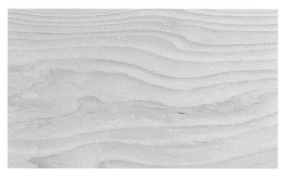

6–74. *Yew* (Taxus baccata)

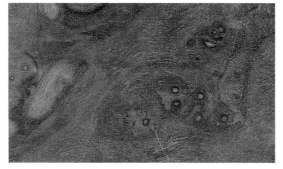

6–71. *Walnut butt*

6–75. *Zebrano* (Microberlinia brazzavillensis)

CHAPTER 7

EXAMPLES OF MARQUETRY

This chapter offers examples of the wide-reaching creative designs possible using marquetry techniques. Illus. **7–2** to **7–12** are examples of the work of some British amateur marquetarians who are members of the Harrow Marquetry Society. Some are relative newcomers to the subject and others are accomplished practitioners of the craft; what they have in common is patience, dedication, and enthusiasm for marquetry in its many forms.

All dimensions given are in inches.

7–1. *"Hydra" (28 x 36) by Arthur Lord, from an original painting by P. D. Breeding–Black, 1987. It is mounted in a conventional picture frame. Notice the artistry that produces the three-dimensional effect.*

7–2. *"Free Spirit" (14 x 21) by Brian Freestone (own composition)*

7–3. *"Riverside" (13.5 x 15.5) by Alan Farquharson (from a painting by unknown artist)*

7–4. *"Old Curiosity Shop" (12.5 x 14.5) by Ronald Newell (from an original by Art Veneers)*

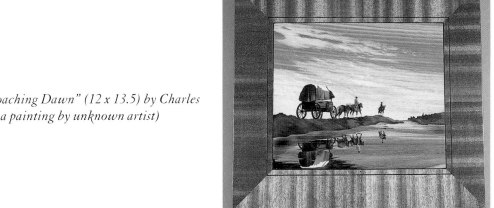

7–5. *"Approaching Dawn" (12 x 13.5) by Charles Good (from a painting by unknown artist)*

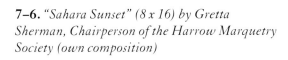

7–6. *"Sahara Sunset" (8 x 16) by Gretta Sherman, Chairperson of the Harrow Marquetry Society (own composition)*

7–7. *"Champagne" (11 x 14) by Anthony Gillette (from an old postcard)*

7–8. *"Playtime with Toby" (10.5 x 13.5) by Joan Phelan (interpreted from a Holly Hobby picture)*

7–9. *"Lost and Found" (10.5 x 13) by Chris Mills (from a Christmas card of unknown origin)*

7–10. *"Summer Idyll" (10 x 11.5) by Jack Roseigh, who produced this original work at the age of 92 (title supplied by the author)*

7–12. *"Tropicana" (6 x 9) by Janet McBain (origin unknown)*

7–11. *"Penny Farthing" by Ronald Newell (from a rubber stamp)*

Part Two:
Inlaying

CHAPTER 8

INTRODUCTION TO INLAYING

Do not labor under the illusion that abbreviated instructions for inlaying, as found in many current manuals, are new. How about this: In the 1903 edition of *The Handyman's Book*, by Paul N. Hasluck, there appear these instructions on inlaying:

"...if the shelves are to be inlaid, prepare a scratch tool of suitable width and run it round the edge as far as the design permits, finishing the remainder, after it has been set out, with chisels or gouges as may be most convenient."

This author suggests it would have been "most convenient" to receive more information. It is likely that the reader will have formed the distinct impression that there is more to the subject than may be contained in a few dozen words.

It is important to define what is meant by "inlaying." Inlaying is not marquetry, in which shapes are cut and layed, with their edges touching, to create a pictorial or decorative effect. Marquetry subjects, complete and free-standing, may be inlaid, of course, in which case, the best may be obtained from both worlds.

Inlaying is the craft of inserting a motif, or object, into a corresponding recess. Whether the recess is excavated to accept a prepared motif, or the motif is shaped to fill an existing recess, although differing in their respective methods, the essential requirement is to create as perfect a match as possible between the two parts.

GROUNDS SUITABLE FOR RECEIVING INLAYS
Types of Ground
The term "ground" refers to whatever is the material, or item, into which the inlay is to be inserted.

Primarily the purpose of the inlay is to enhance the appearance of the object; therefore, its color and texture must be compatible with the ground, together with the coordination of shapes and sizes.

Many types of ground are used, and usually they are associated with a particular object, such as furniture, musical instruments, or other artifacts.

Considering furniture: tabletops, being generally one of the largest and probably plainest items of domestic furniture, are ideal subjects for decoration. Here are opportunities to inlay a central motif and a border string. Whether of one-piece solid construction or a framed panel variety, the motif serves much the same purpose from the inlayer's viewpoint. It would not matter if the top had been veneered, the inlaying technique need not be any different from the application to a solid top, except for the following caveat: normally, after insetting any inlaid decoration, it is necessary to level the components to make a smooth surface. Clearly, there is a limit to how much cutting back can be undertaken with a veneered top; few liberties can be taken in this operation.

Writing slopes were sometimes treated to ornate decoration; some might feel they were a bit overdecorated. Now and then an example appears constructed from excellent material with tasteful ornamentation—maybe an oval motif on the lid, with a corner trimmed in a laminated banding of alternating ebony and sycamore. Likely as not, the writing slope also carries fair specimens of inlaid metalwork, in the way of hinges and catches.

In this case, the material of the ground will almost certainly be solid hardwood, mahogany perhaps, or if it is veneered, then the carcass will be one of the better-quality softwoods. Many modern workshops producing such items use man-made particleboard for very good reasons. The material is easily worked, stable, and inexpensive. Medium density fiberboard, commonly referred to as mdf, is available in sheet form of controlled thickness, with smooth, level surfaces. For those who object to the use of this material suggesting its inferiority to natural wood, I understand that mdf uses material that might otherwise be wasted and, foot for foot, contains more natural fiber than wood itself! Nevertheless, mdf produces dust in large amounts when being machined or abraded and precautions must be taken to protect the respiratory system and eyes with appropriate safety masks and goggles.

Inlaying associates two basic elements: the inlay and the ground into which it will be embedded. Considering the material used to produce the inlaid component, specification depends greatly upon which type of inlay is required. With almost no exception, they are made from hardwoods. Exotic wood of bright, dark, or otherwise spectacular hues are greatly prized, although dyes or stains are used to color common pale hardwoods such as box or sycamore.

Straight components made of square or rectangular sections may be called by any of the following names: banding, binding, stringing or lines.

Banding (**8–2** and **8–9**) is applied in narrow or wide strips to resemble bands of strapping or ribbon. Binding is the name given to the inlaying of the strip that decorates and protects a corner of a box or instrument. Stringing often refers to the ornamental inlay that separates two parts of say, a box lid, or portions of a tabletop. Often inset from the edge of a panel or frame, stringing is generally straight and made up of several veneers embodying a pattern within its structure.

Lines (**8–1** and **8–2**), as the name suggests,

are plain wood sections, normally available in boxwood, rosewood and ebony, in widths from $\frac{1}{39}$ to $\frac{1}{4}$ inch (1 to 6 mm). Dyes are used to stain boxwood and other light woods to produce other colors. Lines are found in borders and edges and usually refer to light-weight sections. But, there is no rigid ruling about these terms; they vary depending on the trade, locality, and item bearing the inlay.

Purfling (**8–1** and **8–4**) is usually made of three laminates of veneer, black-white-black being the most common arrangement, and is a type of inlay associated almost exclusively with the inlaid decoration found in musical instruments of the string family. It may be found around the edges of fronts and backs of most violins, for example. It is not unusual to combine two or more purflings to produce wider inlays, such as may be seen on the corner banding of some guitars.

Rosettes (**8–3**) come in various styles of round motifs, but the most impressive are those that are made especially for the guitar. The sound hole that is a characteristic of the top of the guitar is almost always decorated with a rosette comprising a composition of plain rings from lines or purfling for the outer and inner diametric elements, enclosing so-called "Tunbridge-ware" mosaics. These are most frequently made by specialists and purchased by luthiers for inlaying into sound-boards of instruments of their own making.

Motifs are many and various, not necessarily of a common geometric shape, but often so. Shapes may include roundels, ovals and squares—some with geometric patterns, others with floral or pictorial compositions. Sizes may be as small as $\frac{5}{8}$ inch (15 mm) or over 12 inches (300 mm). Background veneers are usually mahogany or walnut and are available in quantity from veneer houses that specialize in producing a range of designs, some traditional, others of their own patterns.

TYPES OF INLAY

Illus. **8–1** to **8–9** show the variety of inlays possible.

TOOLS AND EQUIPMENT

Tools fall into two basic categories: those used for excavating recesses and those for shaping

INLAYS

8–1. *An assortment of lines, stringing, and purfling showing a range of colors and styles in common use. Lines are usually small, plain, single-color inlays that are square in cross-section. Stringing are inlays made of single or multiple pieces of plain or decorative wood. Purfling is associated with musical instruments. It consists of a central strip contrasting in color to the two outer strips.*

INLAYS (continued)

8–2. *Inlaid borders of lines and banding.*

8–3. *Usually produced for, not by, the luthier, rosettes are a special item in the inlayer's repertoire.*

8–4. *A fine example of three-veneer purfling inlaid superbly into the soundboard of a viol. In some examples—the Maggini violin family for instance—double purfling is a hallmark, with two lines of black/white/black purflings, separated by a small gap.*

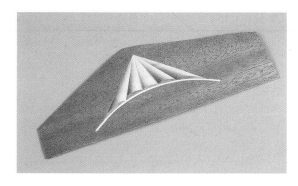

8–5. *A variation on the theme of mock-shading enhances these corner designs. The technique is achieved by placing into hot sand the area to be darkened by partial scorching. (See Chapter 3.)*

INLAYS (continued)

8–6. *Carefully chosen woods with subtle shading are a feature of this inlay, prepared for application as a surface decoration.*

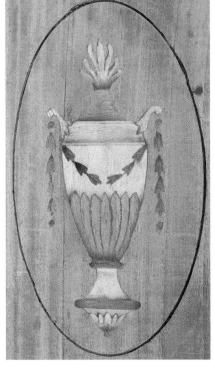

8–8. *Greco-Roman symbols, as depicted in this example, were used frequently to decorate furniture from the 17th to 19th centuries.*

8–7. *A simple but effective design is used for this oval inlay. It is produced by the stack-cutting method with inscribed lines to emphasize the leaf shapes.*

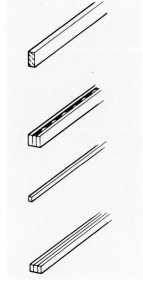

8–9. *Plain or laminated veneers are used to make banding and stringing inlays.*

inlays. Below are the tools necessary to inlaying, not all of which are found in the average tool kit. Other tools such as rulers and other common items, appear where relevant in the text.

Tools for Excavating Recesses
CHISELS AND GOUGES
A selection of chisels and gouges suitable for recessing and trimming are needed **(8–11)**. Chisels are used for: stabbing cuts to define edges and ends of recesses; trimming joints in stringing; and excavating floors of recesses.

Gouges, in small sizes, of the spoon and fish-tail shapes, are used to clear away waste material from bottom faces of recesses.

Toothpick Chisel
A so-called toothpick chisel is used to remove waste from narrow channels and to clean out corners. It is made from a standard 2-inch (50-mm) oval nail, bent after insertion into a wooden handle and shaped on a grindstone to form a chisel point **(8–12** and **8–13)**. It could be done with a file just as effectively. It is useful to have a small selection of widths and end shapes to cope with various contingencies. When it becomes blunt, the nail is replaced with a new one.

CHANNEL CUTTERS
Illus. **8–14** to **8–18** show a variety of channel cutters.

Knives
Illus. **8–19** shows knives used to mark trimming and incising. The first two from the left were made by the author from old cut-throat razors. Craft knives of the type with blades that slide into handles are not suitable owing to the lack of rigidity in the blade fitting. The instability of the design renders the knife prone to wandering.

Customized knives with smooth, bevelless sides for marking around motifs are effective, but, if preferred, the knives demonstrated for marquetry are good for lightweight applications.

Circle Cutter
A circle cutter is used for incising circles, prior to excavating channels **(8–20)**. In this particular tool, the blade is made from a piece of broken file, ground to the correct shape and sharpened to a razor edge.

Intended for the edge-cutting of circles and the inlaying of rosettes and other circular motifs, the circle cutter may also be used for the cutting out of motifs for inlaying. Various models are available which differ in levels of sophistication. The less gadget-ridden, the easier they are to handle, as a general rule. As with all cutting tools, most work well, provided the blades are properly sharpened.

Hand Routers
Hand routers **(8–21)** are sometimes called, rather rudely, "old-woman's tooth," being a small single cutter held in a frame for excavating a fixed and preset depth. As with the circle cutter and related tools, the less complex, the less trouble. The blade, being bent at right angles, is difficult to hold while honing, but perseverance pays great dividends.

Scratch Stock
Illus. **8–22** shows an old hand-made scratch stock made from a piece of much-used elm, proving again that where wood is concerned, there is no such thing as "waste"! A piece of broken hacksaw blade held in place with a

Text Continues on Page 118

Tool Storage

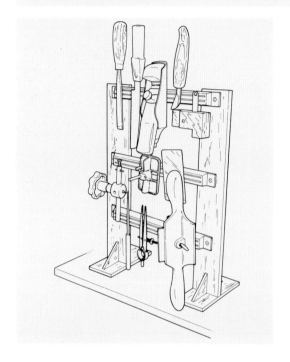

8–10. *Tool storage is an important aspect of craft work. Tools need to be tidy when not in use, but readily available when needed. A rack with magnetic strips, as used to hold knives in a kitchen, may be adapted to function efficiently as a marquetry/inlaying tool stand. On the magnetic rack are the following tools: top row; chisel, saw, plane, and knife; middle row; circle cutter, hand router, and cabinet scraper; bottom row; scraper burnisher, dividers, and two-handed scraper.*

Tools for Excavating Recesses

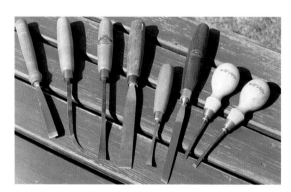

8–11. *A variety of chisels and gouges useful for trimming and recessing.*

8–12. *An oval nail inserted into a wooden handle and bent about 60 degrees.*

8–13. *The head of the nail has been shaped on a bench grinder.*

Tools for Excavating Recesses (continued)

8–14. *This is an example of a refined channel cutter made to the author's specifications by Carl Holtey. Its operation is detailed in Chapter 9.*

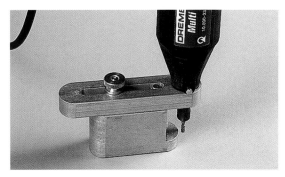

8–17. *The purpose of a channel routing jig, with mini-power tool attached, is to cut channels parallel to a straight or curved edge. Its use is detailed in Chapter 9.*

8–15. *A basic channel cutter is a simple tool that is adjustable for width and depth of cut and easy to apply with one hand.*

8–18. *A traditional pattern-marking-gauge is used for scribing parallel lines along a straight edge. If the scribing point is sharpened, it may also be used to cut banding from veneer sheet.*

8–16. *A barrel-type channel cutter is used with a mini-power tool, which is detailed in Chapter 9.*

8–19. *Knives used to mark trimming and incising.*

TOOLS FOR EXCAVATING RECESSES (continued)

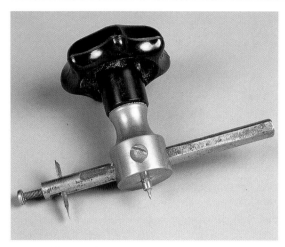

8–20. *This circle cutter is made from a broken file and is used to mark circles prior to excavating channels.*

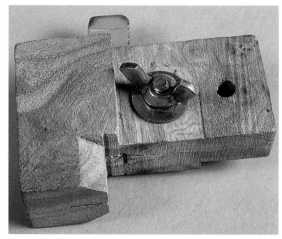

8–22. *This hand-made scratch stock consists of a piece of broken hacksaw blade held in place with a wing nut and bolt.*

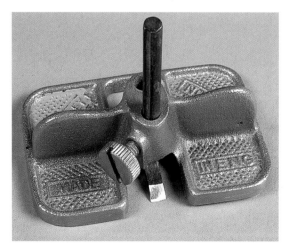

8–21. *Hand routers are used to excavate fixed and preset depths.*

8–23. *A two-handed scraper (top), a flexible cabinetmaker's scraper (bottom left), and a heavier, more rigid type (bottom right).*

Tools for Excavating Recesses (continued)

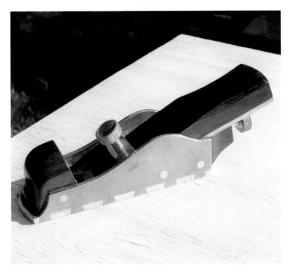

8–25. *A mini-power tool is shown with its router attachment. Speeds from 10,000 to 37,000 rpm drive rotary cutters for a wide variety of applications. The router attachment has a precise adjustment system to permit great accuracy in depth control, and the design of the base allows clear viewing of the work in progress.*

8–24. *This thumb plane, made to the author's specifications by Carl Holtey, was based on a Norris pattern.*

8–26. *A selection of cutters, burrs, and drills used with a mini-power tool. An enormous range of these attachments are readily available.*

wing nut and bolt are all that is necessary to make up this simple but effective tool. The one shown was made by the author in a few minutes about twenty years ago.

SCRAPERS

Scrapers **(8–23)** are marvelous tools for cleaning back inlays and removing superfluous material to create a smooth surface. The uninitiated may find the blade something of a mystery. Advice on the sharpening of the burnisher and its application will be found in Chapter 4.

The two-handed scraper, sometimes called a scraper plane, has the advantage of making surfaces level, as well as smooth. Somewhat tricky to set up, these scrapers are superb tools when the burred edge and blade exposure are set correctly.

PLANES

Any size of smoothing plane may be used for surface leveling and general smoothing prior to the embedding process. The thumb plane shown in **8–24** has a low-angle, extra-hard blade and a very narrow throat to ensure a clean slice with reduced risk of tearing out grain.

Motorized Routers

The router, in a range of sizes, powered by an electric motor, is one of the most common machine tools found in the contemporary workshop. Not surprising, since it is one of the most versatile tools a woodworker may own, with applications for an inlayer, too.

One of the smaller varieties, such as the one shown in **8–25**, is ideal for our purposes, as many useful and appropriate accessories are available to extend its range of application. Router attachments, router tables, and other accessories are available for mini-power tools, as well as a book on the subject by this author, *Mini Power Tool Handbook*.

TOOLS FOR SHAPING INLAYS

Tools for shaping inlays include fretsaws **(8–27)** or scroll saws **(8–28)**, odd-leg dividers or calipers **(8–29)**, stringing thicknesses **(8–30 to 8 –32)**, and vises **(8–33 and 8–34)**. The stringing thicknesser is a purposely made tool for regulating the thickness of stringing or any piece of wood up to about 1/4 inch (6 mm) thick and about 2 inches (50 mm)wide. It is a simple matter to reduce the thickness and smooth the surface of the inlay by passing it between the blade and the table of the thicknesser. It is similar to a spokeshave, but with the work fed in the opposite direction; the inlay is forced through the gap between the blade and the table. Waste is removed by the scraping action. The blade is set to create a slightly larger gap on one side and at a height to admit the stringing in a raw sawn state. As the inlay is gradually drawn past the blade to remove the waste, it is traversed across progressively with each pass toward the side with the smaller gap. Set the adjustment to achieve the required finished thickness of the stringing made with the screw guides. A few passes should ensure a perfectly level and smooth stringing of uniform thickness throughout its length.

SAWS

8–27. *A hand-operated fretsaw used for cutting out motifs. Most people will master the hand-held fretsaw quickly enough to produce intricate motifs from thin wood. Standard saw blades are available internationally, in various specifications, but generally, inlay work demands fine-toothed types.*

8–28. *This is a typical powered scroll saw, representing a modern alternative to the hand-powered fretsaw. Incorporated features include a tilting table, dust blower, variable speeds, and other helpful features. Scroll saws allow a "both hands-on" contact with the workpiece as the blade reciprocates vertically.*

The books Scroll Saw Bench Guide *and* Success with the Scrollsaw, *by this author, demonstrate the application of many models and teach essential techniques.*

CALIPERS

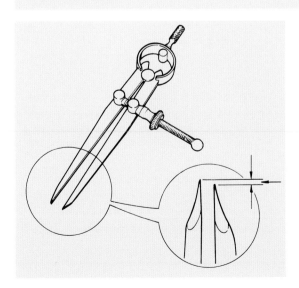

8–29. *Odd-leg dividers or calipers are so-called because the ends of the two legs of the calipers, normally of equal length, are unequal. They are converted from a standard pair of engineer's dividers that have been adapted by reforming the points. One leg is ground shorter than the other, but both legs are sharpened, like knife-blade points, to perform as incisors. They are used for scribing a second line parallel to an existing one by inserting the longer leg into the incision and using the shorter one to mark the second line. The width between the legs is adjusted by rotation of the thumbscrew, and, since the circular hinge is of spring steel, the legs are held securely in position. They are detailed in Chapter 10.*

Using a Stringing Thicknesser

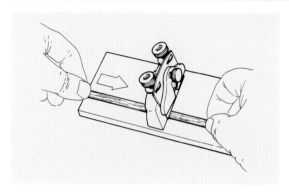

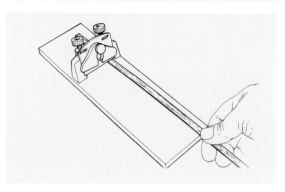

8–30. *A strip of stringing is shown being fed through the gap between the blade and the table on the thicknesser.*

8–31. *Stringing is fed through several times, gradually reducing in thickness as it is passes through and across the table. The gap is smaller on one side to permit a fine graduation of the process.*

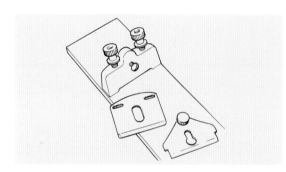

8–32. *Three metal components make up the thicknesser: a cast-metal base, plus the blade and top iron from a spokeshave. The blade edge is relieved at each corner to avoid leaving tramline marks, and it is set to give a slight angled gap above the table to permit gradual thicknessing of the string. The one shown in use was given to the author by Bob Wearing, a craftsman/author and designer of many superb devices.*

Vises

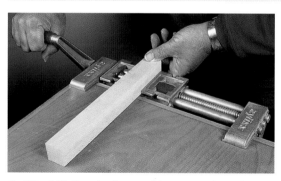

8–33. *A Zyliss vise is a multipurpose clamping system that is attached to a worktop or bench. It is more adaptable than any other type of vise and in the application shown above, it holds the workpiece securely on the worktop, without impeding the tools in use on the surface of the work.*

8–34. *With its rotating and tilting action, the Swivel vise can be locked in almost any position, allowing maximum flexibility of work positioning. Detachable soft jaws are a boon to securing delicate work, and the vise is easily attached to any worktop by its clamp.*

CHAPTER 9

INLAYING CORNER BANDING & STRINGING

PRINCIPLES OF EXCAVATION FOR INLAID MOTIFS

Excavating recesses for inlaying motifs, panels, tablets and the like is different from the methods used for banding, stringing, and lines.

The term "excavate" in respect to the recessing of the ground to receive an inlay is a more accurate term than "create." Even so, some may relate excavation to the more crude "digging" of a hole in the earth.

A recess in the world of the inlayer must be precisely excavated to the measurements of the inlaid item, plus an almost unmeasurably small margin to allow its insertion. With regard to the depth of the inlay, theoretically speaking, the element to be embedded should be inset at as shallow a depth as possible, for the sake of speed and efficiency, among other considerations. It should be remembered that, after embedding, the leveling of the related surfaces is likely to remove some ground and inlay simultaneously. Due allowance must be made when the inlay is being prepared for its embedded depth.

INLAYING CORNER BANDING (1ST METHOD)

Banding, being composed of one or more straight strips of veneer, may also be taken to represent the terms "binding" and "lines." This is setting aside, for the moment, purfling made from three layers of veneer and stringing with "sandwiched" cross-banded decoration within the outer layers.

For the methods shown and described in **9–1** to **9–16**, the Holtey channel cutter is used;

in **9–10** to **9–16**, it is used to inlay a single laminated corner banding. This laminated banding is a strip of three layers in a black-white-black color arrangement. Great accuracy is required in cutting the width of the channel because the layers are very thin, leaving virtually no space for an ill-fitting banding. It is intended to produce a channel fitting the banding so precisely as to require no more leveling than a light smoothing of the related surfaces when fitting is completed. It is wise to carry out a test on an unimportant sample before applying the cutter to the ground chosen for the inlay project.

INLAYING CORNER BANDING (2ND METHOD)

Illus. **9–17** to **9–29** show methods for inlaying corner banding using a cutter in a mini-power tool.

INLAYING CORNER BANDING (3RD METHOD) AND INLAYING STRINGING (1ST METHOD)

From the sophisticated we go to the simple, to demonstrate how, with a little imagination, the equipment needed may be shop-made (**9–30** to **9–38**). But this equipment need not be considered inferior; rather, it should be regarded as custom-built, economic, and, above all, effective.

INLAYING CORNER BANDING (4TH METHOD)

This inlaying method for corner banding described and shown in **9–39** to **9–50** uses a router cutter.

INLAYING STRINGING (2ND METHOD)

Illus. **9–51** to **9–54** show another method of inlaying stringing in which a channel cutter is used to mark the channel and a hand router is used to excavate the waste. String inlay is often associated with furniture, particularly where large areas of plain surfaces need a visual lift, such as a border around a tabletop. A piece of rosewood was selected for this demonstration, to represent part of a traditional item of furniture. The stringing inlay is also traditional in design, that of a black-and-white herringbone pattern enclosed with black lines.

The preparatory step of running a test on a scrap sample was carried out before commencing work on the rosewood, a recommendation emphasized frequently in this book. Incising channels works satisfactorily, as long as the depth of cut is controlled sensitively. The lightest cut is applied first to merely mark the surface, by tilting the tool to permit only partial incision of the blade. Subsequent passes are performed, adjusting the blade angle progressively, increasing the depth of the cut and the downward pressure of the tool.

Parallel cuts are made, like train track lines, to match the width of the stringing, achieved by adjustment of the crossbar holding the blade.

INLAYING STRINGING (3RD METHOD)

Illus. **9–55** to **9–62** describe and show a method of inlaying using a channel-routing jig attached to a mini-power tool.

INLAYING STRINGING (4TH METHOD)

Illus. **9–63** to **9–71** describe and show a method of inlaying stringing using a router base attached to a mini-power tool.

INLAYING USING A CHANNEL CUTTER

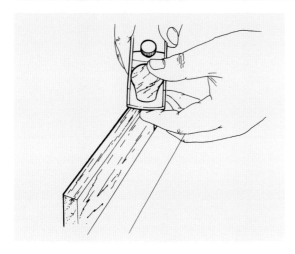

9–1. *Before cutting the channel, it is essential to prepare the edge of the ground. It should be smooth, level and straight, because it will become the reference against which the cutter will be applied. Any irregularity in this edge would be reproduced in the groove.*

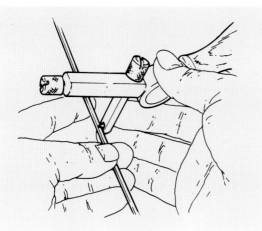

9–2. *A single cutter blade is fitted and set to the depth of the banding. The preliminary requirement is to set the depth of the cutter to match the banding—in this case, a square section. To produce the desired recess, the cutting gauge may be applied with the same setting to both the face and edge of the ground.*

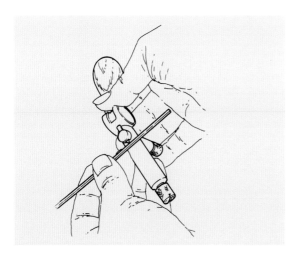

9–3. *Setting the width to suit the banding is done in the same manner as setting the depth. Aim to make the depth of cut slightly more than the depth of the banding, about 5 percent deeper than the banding depth. This is to ensure that when both cuts have been made into the edge and face, the waste will come away cleanly without leaving "crumbs" in the corner.*

INLAYING USING A CHANNEL CUTTER (continued)

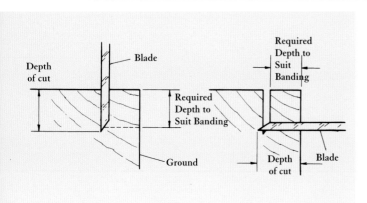

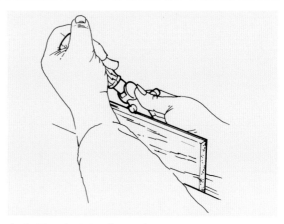

9–4. *This diagram shows the cutting of a corner channel. In the first cut, to establish the width of the cut, the incision is set a little deeper than the banding. In the second cut, the same principle is applied; the depth is set correctly, but the incision is slightly deeper to ensure a rabbet (rebate) with a clean corner.*

9–5. *For the initial cut, the cutting gauge is leaning forward to reduce the penetration of the blade. A more upright angle will be applied gradually until it is vertical, achieving the full depth of incision.*

In situations where a corner banding is to be applied on four sides of a square or rectangular ground, two of the sides will run with the grain and two sides will run across the grain. In the example shown, the grain happens to run with the width, not the length, of the workpiece.

Holding the ground in a vise or some other clamp, the cutting gauge is applied first along the face and then along the edge of the width, that is, across the grain. This sequence is planned so that, with the possibility of the cross-grain breaking out at the ends, such faults will be removed during the cutting of the long-grain sides. The cutting action may be applied in both directions as long as the blade has been prepared correctly. (See Chapter 8.)

Depth of cut is controlled by leaning the handle forward such that only a small amount of the blade is in contact with the surface of the ground, even though the blade is set at full depth. Bringing the handle to the vertical in stages, as each subsequent pass is made, takes advantage of the facility to graduate the rate of incision, thus reducing risk of tear-out.

First cuts should be very light, with the intention of merely marking the line.

9–6. *A waste piece has been cut away from the ground, leaving a clean groove. It is almost identical in section to the ebony banding lying at its side. When full depth is reached, the cutting gauge is applied to the edge in the same manner as that described above, resulting, hopefully, in the removal of a square slip of waste—leaving a clean recess for the application of the corner banding.*

INLAYING USING A CHANNEL CUTTER (continued)

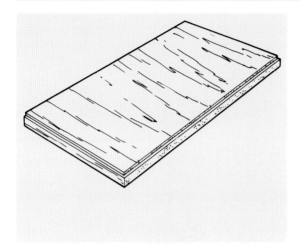

9–7. *Two sides are recessed, awaiting the fitting of the banding. A trial fit of all corner banding on both sides should be carried out to be sure that the channel is the correct size.*

The banding may be cut to length and mitered carefully. After a satisfactory dry fit, the banding may be glued in with any normal woodworking adhesive, and retained until dry under pressure using masking tape.

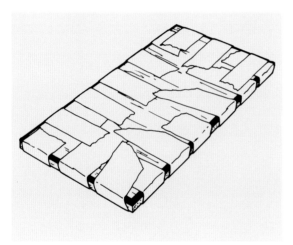

9–8. *Glue is applied thoroughly with light coats to all grooves in the ground, and the corner banding is retained with masking tape. If the depth setting is correct, there should be just a little of the banding to clean up to level it with the ground.*

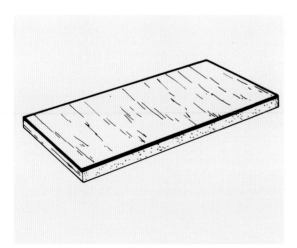

9–9. *To finish the inlaying process, the banding and the ground are scraped clean and level in readiness for the application of varnish or other surface finish.*

INLAYING A SINGLE LAMINATED CORNER BANDING

9–10. *The width between blade and tool fence is set by direct reference to the banding.*

9–11. *This close-up demonstrates how closely the blade and the banding are matched.*

9–12. *A swivel vise is used to hold the short workpiece above the work top to allow freedom of movement of tools and hands.*

9–13. *The second cut is marked or incised into the second side of the workpiece. When the correct depth is reached, the waste will fall away from the channel.*

INLAYING A SINGLE LAMINATED CORNER BANDING

9–14. *Clean edges are evident on all cut faces of the channel and the waste.*

9–15. *Glued and taped in position, the banding is then fitted.*

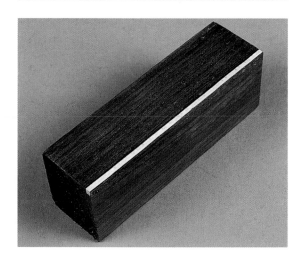

9–16. *A perfect marriage is shown between the workpiece and the corner banding, which is ready for varnishing.*

INLAYING WITH A MINI-POWER-TOOL CUTTER

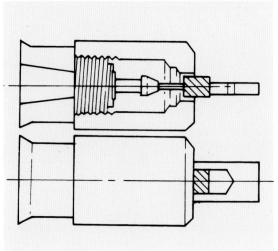

9–18. *The upper view shows a cutaway of the side of the MacDonald binding router attachment. The cutter is wider than the bearing, so it cuts away waste precisely to the extent of its projection. The lower view shows the cutter enclosed by the bearing, giving support and security while resting on the surface of the workpiece.*

Two different-sized guides are available in this routing-accessory kit, permitting the routing of channels from .040 inch (1 mm) to .120 inch (3 mm). Assembly is a straightforward affair, with accuracy assured once it is set up correctly. As always, some trials are recommended on scrap samples before launching into precious workpieces.

9–17. *A router base designed for cutting corner-banding channels is being attached to a mini-power tool. A high-speed cutter is held in the mini-power tool.*

Very few people with an interest in lightweight woodwork or model crafting need an introduction to mini-power tools. A high-speed rotary power tool is capable of performing many tasks when combined with accessories. For this demonstration, a mini-power tool is used in combination with a router attachment, designed exclusively to produce right-angle channels for corner-banding. Developed especially for recessing channels around guitar edges, this assembly is excellent for cutting corner channels in other similar objects, with either straight or curved sides.

INLAYING WITH A MINI-POWER-TOOL CUTTER

9–19. *The correct routing bearing and cutter diameter are selected to match the chosen banding. A short exercise in patient trial and error pays great dividends.*

For the first project, a piece of very ordinary pine is used, not the easiest to inlay since the alternating soft and hard grain tends to cause inconsistency in the progress of the cutter—often accompanied by tearing out of the soft grain. Nevertheless, using a tungsten carbide cutter in the router guide with the mini-power tool rotating at about 30,000 rpm, the recesses are cut precisely, quickly, and cleanly.

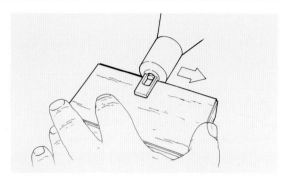

9–21. *The arrow shows the direction of travel during the routing of the channel. In all such freehand routing operations, it is necessary to observe this rule.*

It is worth reemphasizing that it is best to follow the general rule of cutting the cross-grain edges before the long-grain ones, in case of tear-out of the cross grain at the ends. If this happens, then the cutting of the long-grain sides will clean up the broken ends.

9–20. *Cutter projection from the chuck of the mini-power tool is adjusted to suit the depth of the banding.*

The operation of the mini-routing combination is an almost foolproof way of producing a precision recess. For this example, the flat side of the guide is laid on the face of the ground, and, while maintaining contact with the back edge of the guide to act as a fence, the tool is steered along, easily removing waste in a very controlled manner.

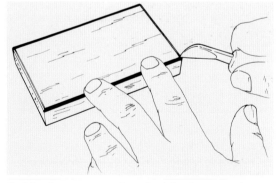

9–22. *Corners are mitered, either by eye or by using a miter gauge, with the intention of making the extreme corners clean and neat. A sharp knife easily chops banding with a downward shearing action.*

INLAYING WITH A MINI-POWER-TOOL CUTTER

9–23. *Care is necessary when establishing the length of the fourth piece of banding, as it must fit the recess and at both ends. No tear-out occurs in the machining of the given example and the recesses are clean and square, with no need of further attention before gluing in the banding. Ebony banding is fitted into the channel with miters cut carefully to produce an attractive decoration on an otherwise commonplace material.*

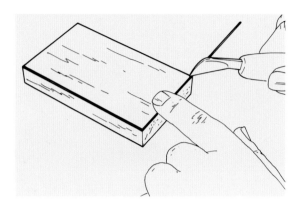

9–24. *All four sides are fitted, glued, and scraped level, creating a framed tablet. Illus. 9–25 to 9–29 show a similar demonstration using the same combination of the mini-power tool and the routing attachment. A different orientation is used, applying the tool vertically rather than horizontally.*

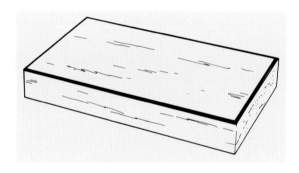

9–25. *To illustrate the effect of incorrect application, the tool is shown traveling in the opposite direction than that recommended. The result is an inconsistent and uneven groove.*

INLAYING WITH A MINI-POWER-TOOL CUTTER

9–26. *A "cleaning" pass is made by returning the tool in the correct direction a couple of times to correct the uneven surface. It may be seen that the opposite top edge has already been inlaid in an earlier project.*

9–27. *As a precaution, the corner of the banding that will be pressed into the corner of the channel is cleaned with a coarse abrasive paper. This ensures that no debris or irregularity will spoil the fitting.*

9–28. *No undue pressure is needed to retain the corner banding in the recess. After gluing, the assembly is held with masking tape.*

9–29. *When the glue is dry, the tape may be removed and the surfaces scraped and smoothed. A light coat of finishing oil has been applied.*

INLAYING CORNER BANDING AND STRINGING WITH SHOP-MADE EQUIPMENT

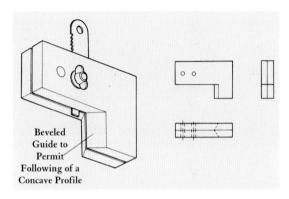

Beveled
Guide to
Permit
Following of a
Concave Profile

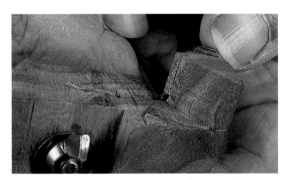

9–31. *It is worth emphasizing the importance of producing a close fit of the blade in its slot. If the fit is not close, there is the risk of wood fibers entering the gap, clogging the joint, and building up debris between the fence, or guide, as it may be called, and the ground. Frequent checks are advised during the scraping process to see that no buildup is occurring.*

Cutters are made from scrap hacksaw blades ground to required sizes; it is best to create a new blade for each string as needed, to provide different sizes that will remain in readiness for further use. Retention of the blade at the correct distance from the fence is achieved by tightening the wing nut on the screw that passes through the two sides of the stock.

Beveling of the fence permits the tool to follow a concave profile, such as a guitar side, just as well as a straight side.

9–30. *The two halves of the scratch stock hold the blade at the required position to produce the correct depth of incision. Two holes are drilled to provide alternative positions for the wing nut and bolt, to permit a choice of blade locations. Here the blade is set to cut a groove for the stringing, not the corner banding.*

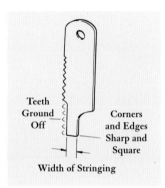

Teeth
Ground
Off

Corners
and Edges
Sharp and
Square

Width of Stringing

9–32. *A scratch-stock blade made from a broken hacksaw blade. Care must be taken to grind the profile while keeping its face square to the edge.*

In application, the scratch stock is gripped in both hands for maximum control, maintaining pressure of the fence against the side of the ground as the ground is traversed in the scraping action. As the stock is pushed forward, it is tilted away for two reasons: to affect the scraping action and to reduce the scraping depth in the early passes. The tool may be used in reverse by pulling, but to function correctly, the tilt must then be toward the operator. A push-pull technique is ideal and not difficult to use.

Progressively, the recess depth is increased and an eye is kept on the uniformity of the channel being produced. Gradually the tool is brought more upright until it is vertical for the finishing passes, when the full depth of the channel is reached. Since many strings are barely thicker than a postcard, very few passes of the scratch stock are necessary to achieve sufficient depth.

Some may prefer to use a tool such as the special Holtey channel cutter to mark and delineate the channel sides prior to scratching out the recess. This is fine if working in a soft ground or one with a wild grain.

INLAYING CORNER BANDING AND STRINGING WITH SHOP-MADE EQUIPMENT (continued)

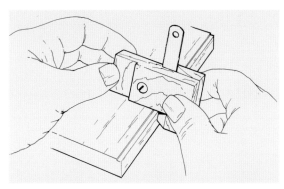

9–33. *The workpiece is fixed securely and the scratch stock is applied by leaning it at a slight angle as it is pushed along with the blade in direct contact with the surface. The cutter is guided by pressing the scratch-stock fence against the side of the workpiece during the operation.*

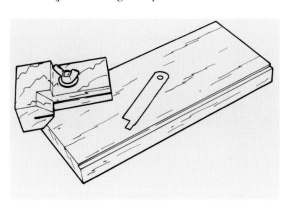

9–34. *A clean rabbeted corner is produced by the scratch stock, which is shown with its blade removed, ready to be reassembled to cut the channel for stringing.*

In the given example, the corner banding is fitted first. The scratch stock is used to cut the recess for both corner banding and stringing, with the same blade as will be used to produce the channel recess.

It is best to fit the corner banding before continuing with the cutting of the recess for the string, since this will protect the edge and give a secure bearing for the fence. Gluing and fixing with masking tape prior to cleaning up with a scraper is the next stage.

9–35. *Here is shown a similar operation to fit a corner banding in another item. It illustrates the application of the scratch stock on the opposite hand from the previous example.*

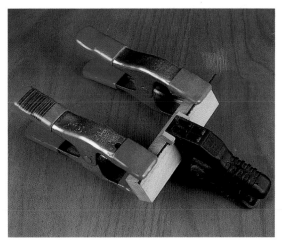

9–36. *Instead of masking tape, three small spring clamps are applied to hold the banding in position while the glue dries.*

Inlaying Corner Banding and Stringing with Shop-Made Equipment (continued)

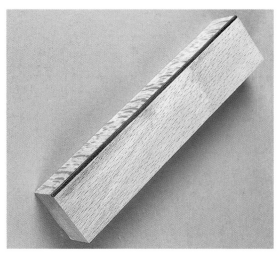

9–37. *Ready for varnishing, the banding is leveled and smooth. Proceeding with the inlaying of the stringing is an operation almost identical to that of embedding the corner banding. Of course, the blade width needs to be checked on a piece of scrap, and care must be taken in setting the required distance from the fence. In the given example, a strip of the ground is left as a spacer between the corner banding and the stringing.*

Width to suit the stringing is merely a question of experimenting to determine a fit between the stringing and the recess. When the adhesive is applied, it may have the effect of swelling the fibers of the inlay. Thus, if there is much of a delay before fitting, there could be a problem due to the expansion of the string spoiling what should be a close fit in the test stage. Any liquid adhesive potentially might expand wood fibers, and that could work in favor of the inlaying process in principle, providing that, after adding the glue, the time in embedding is kept to a minimum.

9–38. *An additional string is added to the soft-wood block after the corner banding is glued. Its groove is produced with the scratch stock in the same manner as for the corner-banding recess. The cutter is ground to match the width of the string.*

When applying the glue, it should be noted that, in the case of a string or other embedded inlay enclosed within a channel, there is the tendency for the glue to act as an air seal and hinder the embedding. Generally this need not be a problem if the glue is spread along the floor of the channel and not the sides. The embedding of the inlay will then force the glue up the sides without hitting a "cushion" of air.

As previously suggested, the string and the surface of the ground may be leveled with a scraper and cleaned up ready for varnishing.

INLAYING CORNER BANDING WITH A ROUTER CUTTER

9–39. *This method uses a router cutter whose design incorporates a pilot bearing. As may be seen, at the end of the cutter is the pilot, a plain shank that is brought against the edge of the ground to limit the depth of cut. In effect, as long as the cutter is held upright, the depth of cut cannot exceed that of its blade width. The cutter is chosen for its proximity in size to the corner banding. Any inequality of size may be adjusted by leveling the components after the fitting of the banding.*

9–40. *A mini-power tool is used to drive the cutter for this operation. Here the cutter is being installed into the chuck.*

9–41. *Attached to the mini-power tool is a router base whose position is adjustable relative to the mini-power tool. Adjustment of the cutter projection, through the router base, is made to equal the depth of the banding.*

INLAYING CORNER BANDING WITH A ROUTER CUTTER

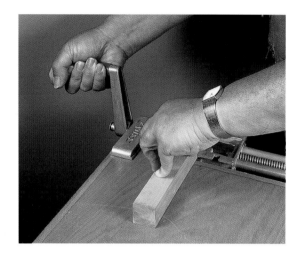

9–42. *Security of the workpiece on top of the bench is achieved with the Zyliss vise.*

9–43. *High revolutions are characteristic of the mini-power tool, and, in cutting the routed groove cleanly, the pilot guide on the cutter actually scorches the side of the ground. No permanent damage is caused, however; the mark is removed with a few strokes of a scraper.*

9–44. *Woodworking adhesive is applied to the groove.*

INLAYING CORNER BANDING WITH A ROUTER CUTTER

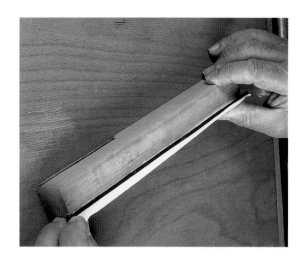

9–45. *Adhesive tape is added to retain the banding during the drying time.*

9–46. *No attempt is made to cut the banding to a suitable length to fit the ground at this stage.*

9–47. *After removing the tape from the glued banding, the length is trimmed and the assembly is held in the vise for leveling, first with the scraper.*

INLAYING CORNER BANDING WITH A ROUTER CUTTER

9–48. *When the leveling of the banding and the ground is accomplished with the scraper, a fine abrasive is used to smooth the surface.*

9–49. *Each side of the assembly is treated similarly.*

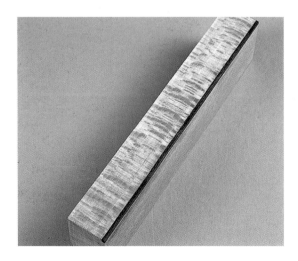

9–50. *The inlay completed with a surface treatment of finishing oil.*

INLAYING STRINGING WITH A CHANNEL CUTTER AND HAND ROUTER

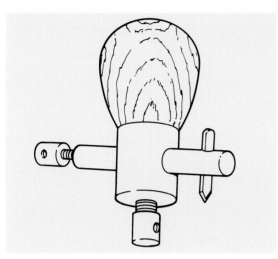

9–51. *Brass was used for the metal parts of this simple but effective channel cutter. The blade may be fixed at the desired depth by the end screw in the cross-bar. Tightening the lower screw clamps the cross-bar to hold the blade at the required distance from the central bar. The latter member is, effectively, the fence.*

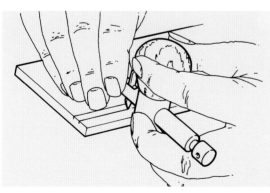

9–52. *Parallel cuts are marked into the ground to act as outlines of the channel in readiness for the excavation.*

Excavation of the waste is then carried out with the hand router, removing a thin sliver of material to test for precise location of the channel. If resistance is felt during any of the incising or excavating processes, relieve the stress by adjusting the blade to a shallower cut.

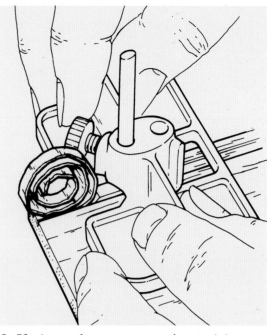

9–53. *A secondary cut removes the remaining waste with one unbroken shaving to reach the desired depth of the excavation.*

Following the cutting of the channel sides, the recess is excavated with the hand router. Care is taken in the setting of the blade depth to leave virtually nothing to remove in the operation to level the surface.

No other work on the channel should be necessary, apart from brushing it out as a cleaning precaution to remove dust prior to gluing in the string.

9–54. *Clean joints and contrasting materials give a bright and effective border to the item.*

INLAYING STRINGING WITH A CHANNEL-ROUTING JIG

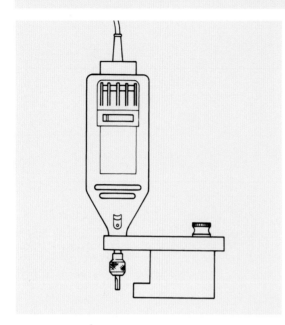

9–55. A straight-sided router cutter is fitted into the chuck of the mini-power tool and the channel-routing jig is attached, ready for channeling.

Developed for the routing of purfling channels in violin soundboards, or for sound-hole inlays in guitars, or for any other operation where channels are required close to an edge, the channel-routing jig is superb. Ideally combined with a mini-power tool for which it was designed, the assembly is quick, easy and efficient.

One of the advantages of mini-power tools is their capacity to drive rotary cutters at speeds in excess of 30,000 rpm, guaranteeing a clean incision, even with softwoods. A piece of old pine with very wide soft grain was chosen to demonstrate this capacity. Into this ordinary material is to be inlaid a piece of delicate stringing of cross-banded tulipwood enclosed in alternate lines of ebony and boxwood.

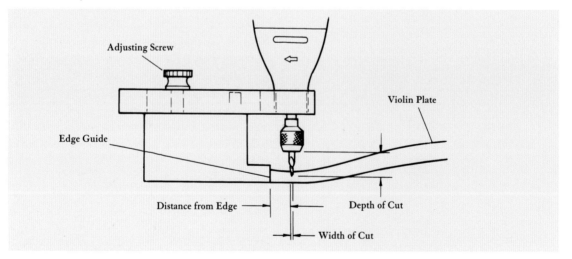

9–56. One possible application of the channel-routing jig is that of incising a groove in a violin top or back, in readiness to receive a purfling inlay. A small amount of adjustment is available to meet the normal needs of inlay depth by adjusting the amount the cutter projects from the chuck. By slackening the adjusting screw on top of the jig, the distance may be adjusted between the edge of the workpiece and the channel.

A cutter of suitable diameter to match the stringing is mounted in the chuck and set to protrude the correct distance to suit the depth of channel. Sliding the tool-carrier to the desired position and locking it with the adjusting screw on top of the jig permits adjustment of the distance between the cutter and the edge of the workpiece. All of the foregoing settings are verified on a test piece, as always, before operating on the workpiece.

INLAYING STRINGING WITH A CHANNEL-ROUTING JIG

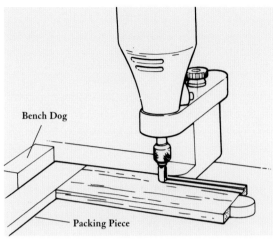

Bench Dog

Packing Piece

9–57. *A packing piece is placed between the clamp and the workpiece to permit access of the cutter. A conventional bench dog is being used here, but any clamping equipment will work as long as it allows freedom to move the jig. (Hands are not shown and the process has been halted for illustration purposes.)*

To perform the channel-routing operation, it is best to clamp the workpiece onto the bench top with space to access the jig. The base of the jig is in contact with the bench top to control the depth of cut as the jig is traversed along the part to be recessed.

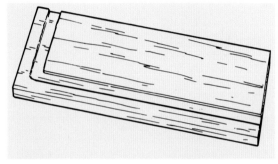

9–58. *Because of the rotation of the cutter, it follows that the outer edges of the corners of the channel will be radiused. These will be squared later. Ragged edges left from the cutter on the surface will come clean after leveling.*

It was decided to cut across the grain, as well as with it, to produce a corner stringing decoration as might be found in a lid or a box top. With the speed set at about 30,000 rpm, the cutter removed waste cleanly without burning or tearing. Any slight burr adhering to the top of the edge will be easily removed during the leveling operation.

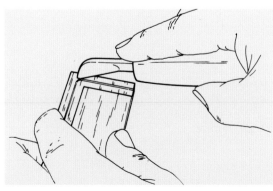

9–59. *At the intersection of the two channels, the radius left in the corner is trimmed out square with a down-cutting action with a sharp knife.*

INLAYING STRINGING WITH A CHANNEL-ROUTING JIG

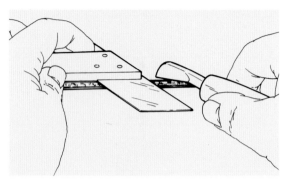

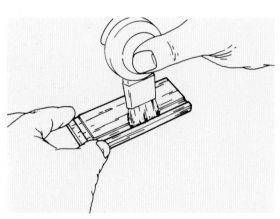

9–60. *Before proceeding with the embedding, the channel is brushed out, to ensure no crumbs are left from the routing to impede the operation.*

9–61. *In order to ensure clean corner joints of the stringing, a miter guide is used to cut the lengths. A miter guide and knife are used to cut the ends of the tulipwood stringing at 45 degrees and to the correct length. Cutting the length accurately is a matter of simply matching the stringing to the length of the channel and marking with a tiny knife cut. Razor-sharp knives are necessary, as always, for this type of cutting.*

Glue is brushed along the bottom of the channel and the stringing inserted and retained with masking tape until the glue is set. Leveling is carried out as usual, with a scraper and fine abrasive paper.

9–62. *Even common softwood may be enhanced with a well-inlaid decorative stringing.*

INLAYING STRINGING USING A ROUTER BASE

9–63. *This method of inlaying stringing uses another combination of tools: a router base attached to a mini-power tool. In the following demonstration, a cutter is used to cut a channel wider than itself by making two cuts side by side.*

9–66. *A measurement is made to place the stringing at the required distance from the edge of the workpiece. For this, the depth gauge on a vernier caliper is used.*

9–64. *Adjustment of the cutter depth and its distance from the fence are features of this multi-purpose accessory.*

9–67. *With the workpiece securely clamped, the first pass is made with the routing assembly. Because the stringing is so slender, the cut is made and the channel depth is achieved in one pass. A repeat pass in the opposite direction serves to clean the channel of any debris and minor imperfections.*

9–65. *Adjustment of the projection of the cutter is made to match the thickness of the stringing itself as a reference to set the cutting depth for the channel.*

INLAYING STRINGING USING A ROUTER BASE (continued)

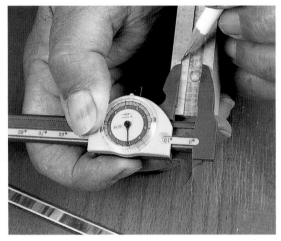

9–68. *A second measurement is made to mark on the workpiece the width of the inlay.*

9–70. *A test is carried out to check the fit of the stringing and, provided all is well, glue is brushed into the channel and the stringing fitted and taped until the glue is dry.*

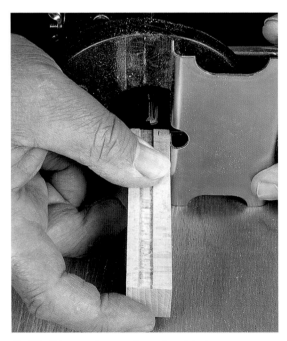

9–69. *Direct reference is made with the cutter aligned to the mark on the workpiece and the router fence is adjusted to suit the new position. The second cut to widen the channel can then be made.*

9–71. *Leveled, smoothed and varnished, the stringing is securely and prettily inlaid.*

CHAPTER 10

INLAYING A RECTANGULAR PANEL

A rectangular panel is a typical subject for inlaying. Panels may be long, short, wide, or narrow. For the demonstration depicted in **10–1** to **10–7**, the panel is about as big as a postage stamp and of solid hardwood about $\frac{1}{32}$ inch (1 mm) thick.

It follows that as the panel has three dimensions—length, width and depth—so must the recess into which it will be fitted. Without wishing to make a laboriously obvious statement, each dimension of the panel must match each dimension of the recess. Clearly, the only facet of the panel that will be visible, following the successful completion of the operation, is its top surface. A close fit between the sides and ends of the panel and the excavated recess is therefore of the greatest importance. Any thought that glue and varnish may make up for discrepancies of fit between the panel and the recess should be abandoned immediately. Such considerations are detrimental to the development of a precise technical discipline. To measure, mark, and cut with optimum accuracy should become the normal aspiration of any craftsperson and, of the inlayer, in particular. The initial objective is to produce, in the ground, a "negative," or upside-down replica of the panel.

A ground of solid hardwood is selected for its appearance and workable characteristics. First we place the panel on the ground at the predetermined location chosen for its final resting place. It is possible to measure the block and transfer the measurements to the ground, but this is not recommended, since fatal errors may occur in the process. Slight inaccuracies in measuring, coupled with possible inexact transference of angles, will lead to unacceptable gaps. It is probably unnecessary to remind the inlay student that discrepancies occurring in the cutting of the recess cannot be readily corrected, particularly if too much material has been removed from the length or width.

It is possible to estimate the depth of the blade insertion in the ground by observing the width of the cut at its point of entry. A tapered blade will show a wider cut the deeper it is inserted. This method of depth assessment becomes more reliable with practice, and, hopefully, the inlayer will benefit from this before launching an attack into precious materials.

Cutting continues to deepen the peripheral cut to a little more than the finished depth of the recess. This is to make sure that when "bottoming out" the recess, there will be less likelihood of ragged corners or fibers adhering untidily to the edges. The knife operation is completed by ascertaining that the corners are well defined, by "stab cutting" them with the knife. This merely requires the placing of the point of the blade, or edge of a chisel, into the corner and pressing downward to ensure that full depth is achieved. Stab-cut both sides of each corner.

Excavation may now begin by applying a keenly sharpened bevel chisel to the task of "ditching" the recess. This term refers to the process of making a small groove around the periphery of the recess to define its edge and depth before leveling the floor. It somewhat resembles the ditch around the sides of a field. Two chisels would be ideal, one to match the width and the other to match the length of the recess. If one's kit does not have these chisels, use a chisel of less width. Trying to make do with one that is even the smallest fraction bigger by skewing it at an angle is courting disaster, because the fine

top edge of the excavation may be so easily destroyed by the shortcomings of inelegant manipulation of the chisel. A knife may be used to create the ditch by slicing along the edge on the waste side of the course, but the knife lacks the required control in this application.

It is recommended to cut the ditches at the ends first, because the first ditching cuts are made in the direction of the grain. Try to judge the angle to remove material to the required depth of the recess. If unsure, then err on the shallow side, since rectification would be merely a matter of taking subsequent slices.

As the chisel is driven in, beware of the temptation to pry out the chip before the cut is completed. If there is the feeling of stubbornness and the chip has not come away when the vertical outlining cut is reached, then the probability is that the knife used for the outlining of the recess achieved insufficient depth. If a prizing action is used in this situation, there is every chance that a split will occur.

To level the floor, at least three methods are available. The most basic is to use the same chisel(s) used for the ditching, applied with the bevel down to remove the waste. Chisels with slightly curved blades lend themselves to accessing the floor and corners of the recess (**10–6** and **10–7**). This requires some skill in the manipulation of the chisel since it is controlled by manual dexterity alone.

A visual guide is provided by the depth of the ditching. Checking frequently for depth may be carried out with the depth gauge on the caliper.

A secondary method and, in my opinion, a superior one, is to use a hand router for the floor leveling. This splendid tool, as was seen in previous examples, will level and set the correct depth simultaneously. The depth

INLAYING A RECTANGULAR PANEL

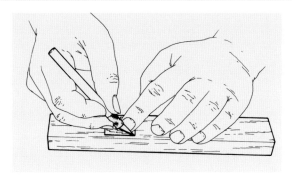

10–1. *Having positioned the panel, a slender, pointed craft knife is applied to mark the outline of the ground around the panel. It is best to hold the panel in place with a clamping device, or even a dab of glue, to ensure its security temporarily during the marking operation. Acquiring the skill for the meticulous application of a knife blade is worth some detailed practice, a prerequisite of which, however, is the acquisition of the correct knife. It is recommended that if the reader has not already done so, then he should refer to the section Tools and Equipment (on pages 110 to 120) before continuing.*

10–2. *A clearly defined edge is made, but it is not yet deep enough to proceed with excavation.*

When using the knife for the marking, or for the initial cut, it is best to mark from the corners toward the middle of each side, to avoid an undesirable slip into an "untouchable" area. This marking cut need not be deep, since its purpose is literally to outline the block. Mistakes may occur if this first cut is performed with more effort than is necessary, since the virgin ground is likely to resist impetuous fumbling and deflect the blade from the intended direction.

When cutting in the direction of the grain, the tendency will be for the blade to follow the soft grain between hard grain lines, as a train follows its tracks. That is fine, if the soft grain is straight and aligned with the required cut. Such good fortune is almost unheard of. Much more likely is that the grain almost follows the direction of the cut, with hard grain deviating and crossing the line, making a tricky job of steering the blade. All the more reason to emphasize the need for a sharp blade, coupled with the lightest application, for the first cut.

Even after establishing the line, caution is recommended for several subsequent cuts, because errors may still occur if one relaxes concentration.

Marking across the grain is easier to manage, provided, to repeat the rule, the light touch is maintained. The alternate soft and hard grain will be readily felt as the knife traverses, and if too hard a pressure is exerted, the hard grain will be crushed and splayed—leaving a crumbling edge that will spoil a clean marriage with the edge of the panel.

Reminder, continue to work from corners to the center of the lines.

Having secured the marking of its periphery, the panel may be removed and set aside. A soft pencil is used to mark the panel and the ground to ensure correct orientation for fitting later.

INLAYING A RECTANGULAR PANEL (continued)

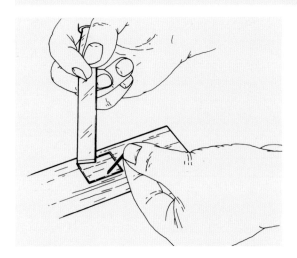

10–3. *"Ditching" the outline of the excavation using a chisel beveled on both sides.*

Deepening of the peripheral cut may now be undertaken by directly inserting the blade into the cut, which is used as a guide. The knife that was used for marking is probably adequate for this job.

We are now concerned with producing the correct depth to suit the thickness of the panel. At this point, an indispensable device is the vernier caliper.

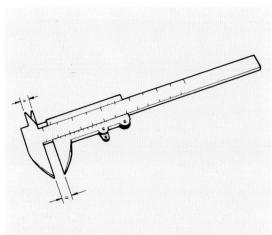

10–4. *A vernier caliper is shown with its three measuring functions: internal and external jaws, plus a depth gauge on the end.*

When the caliper is closed on the panel to measure its thickness, it automatically extends its depth gauge by the same amount. This may be used effectively to visualize the depth required for entry of the knife blade, and later to measure the depth of the recess.

10–5. *Successful ditching outlines the periphery of the recess in preparation for the process of leveling the bottom of the recess.*

INLAYING A RECTANGULAR PANEL (continued)

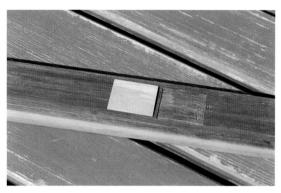

10–7. Excavation of the recess is completed and its match with the panel checked carefully.

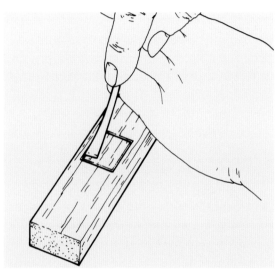

10–6. When the ditching is completed on all four sides, the deepening and leveling of the recess floor can be undertaken with a slightly bent fishtail chisel. The likelihood is that, following the insertion of the panel, the two components, insert and ground, will not be perfectly level. Rather than leave to chance this important feature, it is best to aim to leave the panel slightly protruding, because obviously, it is easier to level the panel to the ground, than the other way around. The floor of the recess must therefore be of such depth as to leave the embedded panel slightly high. The panel needs to protrude no more than paper thickness above the surface of the ground for the leveling process.

10–8. Glued and taped in place, the inlaid panel is then clamped until the glue has dried thoroughly.

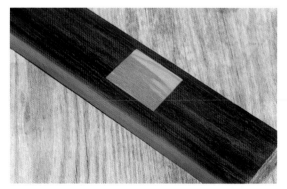

10–9. A scraper was used to level the surface after the glue had set. A rub with oil enhanced the grain of both ground and inlay.

gauge on the vernier caliper may be used for setting the protrusion of the blade in the router. Blade protrusion may be extended progressively, working on the principle that "a little, often" is generally better than one indiscreet hack.

A third method is to use a small power router that may seem to the uninitiated a rather brutal piece of equipment (refer to **11–2** and **11–3** on page 152). It is in fact not much different in size to the average electric shaver and capable of very refined work. Some of the best inlaying ever seen by the author was produced with such a tool, by a luthier who inlays mother-of-pearl decorations into fingerboards for musical instruments. Applications of the machine router are dealt with in other chapters.

EMBEDDING THE MOTIF

To test for a fit, the panel is merely placed over the recess, with an all-round inspection, but not pressed home because of probable difficulty in removing it. It is best if just one gentle trial is attempted, without adhesive, to ascertain the accuracy of the fit, or lack of it. If the match is satisfactory, the panel may now be inlaid.

As with other embedding, glue is spread lightly on the floor of the recess, allowing the easy insertion of the panel without fear of an air lock or bubble. Excess glue will escape from the edges and ensure a secure fixing for the motif. Fix the panel with tape and a clamp, suitably cushioned to avoid damaging it **(10–8)**. When the surfaces of the inlay and the ground are dry, they are scraped level **(10–9)**, smoothed with an abrasive paper, and treated with a suitable oil finish.

TROUBLESHOOTING

If the recess is deeper than the panel, it is possible to glue a sublayer onto the floor of the recess beneath the panel to compensate. One option is to attach, with adhesive, a layer of veneer to the underside of the panel, achieving the same result.

If the recess is too wide, by, say, the thickness of a thumbnail or less, it may be possible to compress the panel in a vise or by hammering. While caution must be exercised during this operation to avoid overstressing the panel, the width may be increased appreciably. Not so the length; that will remain virtually unaltered.

Soaking the panel in water will also increase its width, but there is no guarantee that it will not shrink later.

Another way of correcting excess width is by packing the sides of the recess with veneer, or alternatively, attaching veneer to the sides of the panel. The packing material may be taken from scrap retrieved from the ground. This is harder to achieve if the length of the recess is oversize because this calls for a cross-grain packing and is therefore difficult to cut and to match. The best way is to cut a cross-grain piece of, say, twice the required size—and trim it back to size, after attaching it to the panel with adhesive.

None of the above methods is as good as starting from scratch with a fresh ground, but that may not always be possible.

When leveling the recess floor, it may be necessary to use a router blade with a more pointed edge in order to clear the more intricate corners. If this presents a problem, it is possible to tease out those less accessible portions with the toothpick chisel mentioned earlier.

CHAPTER 11

Inlaying Motifs with Curved or Irregular Shapes

The previous chapter dealt with recessing to suit a rectangular motif. Other shapes, less formal and without straight lines, are dealt with similarly, but more care is needed at the marking-out stage. In the following demonstration (**11–1** to **11–7**), the aim is to inlay an oval motif of floral marquetry into a piece of Brazilian rosewood selected as the ground.

Caution when initiating the marking cut cannot be overemphasized, because the curving lines are sometimes crossing grain at an angle, and sometimes in the direction of the grain. It is the lack of consistency in the travel of the blade as it encounters different grain conditions that creates the problem of directional control. There will probably be an advantage in changing the direction of the blade from time to time, depending on this situation.

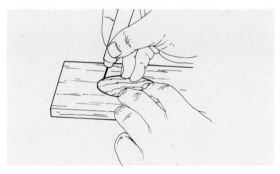

11–1. *Tracing the edge of the motif with a needle point. An almost upright needle is held snug into the corner of the motif and the ground to create an accurate outline.*

This type of motif is sold with a protective backing paper. It is possible to embed the motif with the paper backing uppermost, and remove it in the leveling operation after the inlaying is finished. The marking and subsequent excavation must be produced without reversing it, because the motif may not be symmetrical.

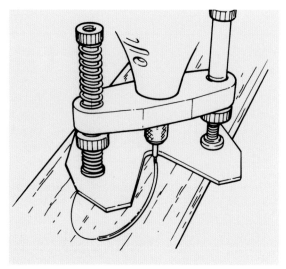

11–3. *Accurate depth of cut is achieved by the fine adjustment available with the router base. Clean excavation is a feature of this tool; uniform depth is a by-product.*

Begin by lowering the rotating cutter bit close to and inside the marked line. The wide aperture in the base of the tool allows constant visual contact throughout the routing procedure. Initially the periphery of the motif is traced at the required depth, leaving only the slightest amount of waste inside the line to be cleared on the second pass.

When cleaning up close to the line, it is best to perform this as one continuous sweep, to avoid inconsistency produced by reentries or restarts. Not easy, but with a bit of practice on a scrap sample, it is achievable.

Having created a ditch around the oval, it is a simple matter to remove the rest of the waste, but best to be methodical. Enlarge the ditch with oval sweeps to leave clearance for the cutter, before working from side to side. Scrupulous care is needed to overlap cutter tracks to leave the floor as flat as possible.

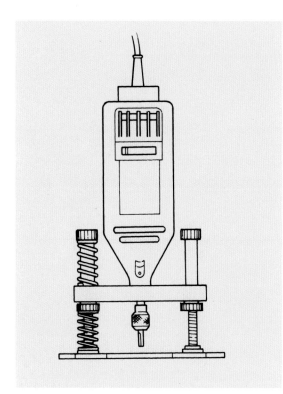

11–2. *For the excavation of the recess, a router base is attached to a mini-power tool by screwing it onto the threaded nose. A fine cutter of small diameter is fitted in the chuck of the mini-power tool. A very large choice of cutters is available, but the ones described as "down-cut" bits are best for recessing and floor leveling, because they leave a clean-cut face.*

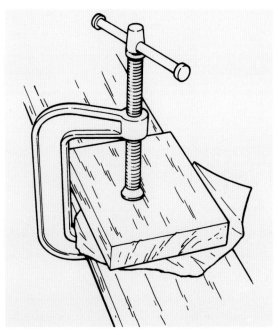

11–4. *Gentle tests with careful inspection are carried out by lowering the motif over the recess.*

Before gluing in the motif, flatness and uniform depth of the recess floor is achieved by scraping, to ensure the level and secure embedding of the motif. Adhesive is lightly painted into the recess and the motif is pressed home. A waste-paper pad covers the assembly and a wooden clamping plate is applied with pressure from a clamp.

11–5. *Between the clamp jaws are the ground with the inlay embedded, a covering waste-paper pad, and a wooden clamping plate.*

After sufficient time has elapsed to ensure the setting of the adhesive, the clamping assembly is dismantled and a thorough inspection is carried out to see that the inlay is secure. Leveling of the surface may then be commenced. Only the very slightest thickness of the inlaid motif should project above the ground surface, if the work was correctly embedded. There will probably be some bits of the waste-paper pad adhering to the motif, confirming the need to avoid the accidental gluing of the motif to the clamping plate. A scraper is probably the best tool to clean back and level the surface. Gradually, the protective backing will come away to reveal the motif.

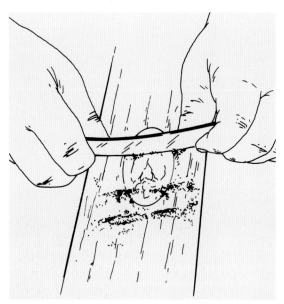

11–6. *It is prudent to scrape with sensitivity to avoid tearing the motif.*

11–7. *A perfect fit! Nominally oval, the inlaid motif may be seen to be symmetrically imperfect, not that it matters, but it emphasizes the need to outline the recess accurately, using the motif as a guide.*

CHAPTER 12

INLAYING A CIRCULAR MOTIF

This chapter demonstrates how to inlay a circular motif into a hardwood ground (**12-1** to **12-16**). A sharp knife is used to mark the outline of the motif onto the ground and to make orientation marks on the ground and inlay, and a router base fitted to a mini-power tool is used in excavating the recess. The depth gauge on the router base is helpful when setting the router depth. The surfaces of the motif and the ground are cleaned up with a scraper.

12–1. *Bought from an inlay supplier, the circular motif is inlaid into a hardwood ground.*

12–2. *A sharp knife is used to mark the outline of the circular motif that has been attached temporarily with adhesive to the ground. Because the backing paper will be left uppermost, when the motif is fitted, the glue is applied to its front.*

12–3. *Orientation marks are made on both the ground and the inlay to ensure correct location when the embedding is carried out.*

12–4. *Conventional wood glue is used, and this releases easily with a thin knife after the marking is completed. The marking process takes only a few minutes.*

12–5. *After the glue is released from the motif, the incised mark is clearly viewable.*

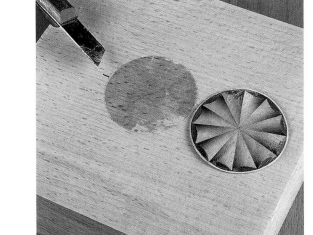

12–6. *A simple routing base is fitted to a mini-power tool to excavate the recess.*

12–7. *Part of the router base incorporates a depth gauge, to assist when setting the routing depth.*

12–8. *To ensure a clean cut, a down-cutting router bit is loaded into the chuck and the router base is attached to complete the assembly.*

12–9. *Depth setting of the cutter is verified by a test cut performed on a scrap block.*

12–10. *The motif is placed on a flat surface, and the block with the test recess is applied to the motif. After some trial and error, a desirable depth is reached, with the intention to produce a slight projection of the motif over the ground surface.*

12–11. *To remove the glue from the work surface while avoiding the risk of clogging the cutter flutes, a damp cloth is applied to the surface. This also helps to soften the fibers to ease the process of incising the hard ground.*

12–12. *The router base has apertures to permit clear viewing of the routing operation. Work from the edge of the recess toward the center and go back to refine the edge last of all. The intention is to clear the material from the recess, up to, and just touching, the incised outline.*

12–13. *With the prescribed marks on the ground and the motif matching, adhesive is brushed lightly into the recess and a waste-paper sheet is placed under the clamping board.*

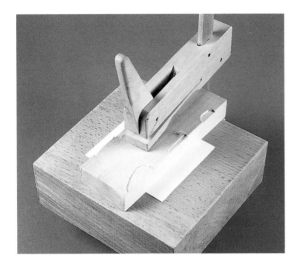

12–14. *A strong clamp is applied for the required setting time of the glue.*

12–15. *The customary treatment is given with a scraper to level and clean up the surfaces of the motif and the ground.*

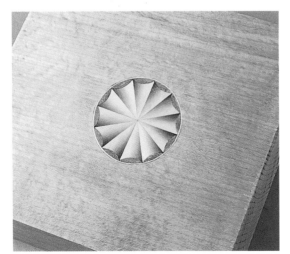

12–16. *The inlaying is complete and the work-piece is ready for surface treatment.*

CHAPTER 13

CREATING A MOTIF & INLAYING IT

The illustrations in this chapter demonstrate how to create your own motif and inlay it. A fretsaw is used to cut the motif outline, which is attached to the inlay material with masking tape. A piece of carbon paper is used on top of the inlay material underneath the design. This prevents the edges of the pattern from becoming ragged, which would occur if a paper copy were used. As was the case in the previous chapter, a router base attached to a mini-power tool is used to excavate the recess. The shell-design convolutions are incised with a knife and emphasized with a ballpoint pen.

13–1. *A design is either created or chosen from an existing source and is drawn or copied onto paper.*

13–2. *To prevent its moving during transfer to the workpiece, the design is fixed along one edge of the inlay material with masking tape. A piece of carbon paper is placed on top of the material underneath the design.*

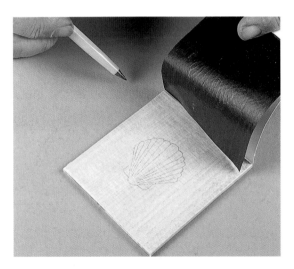

13–3. *A ballpoint pen is used to trace over the outline of the design to transfer its complete details onto the material chosen for the motif.*

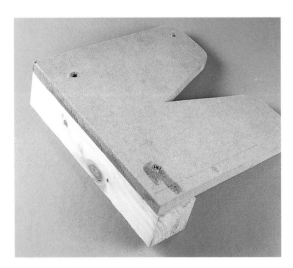

13–4. *A fretsaw table will be clamped to the worktop in readiness for the sawing out of the motif.*

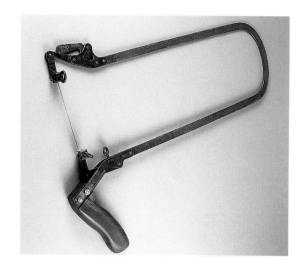

13–5. *A fine old fretsaw by Hobbies—owned by the author since he was a child—has a blade-tensioning device and various adjustments to assist in efficient operation. Sad that this model is no longer available.*

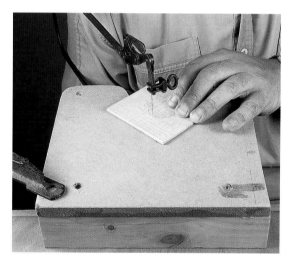

13–6. *Fretsawing the outlined motif. The reason for the carbon copy is to avoid the risk of making the edges of the pattern ragged if a paper copy were used.*

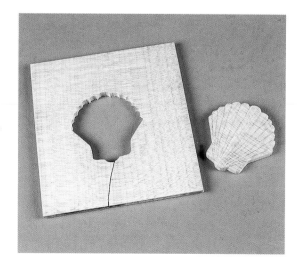

13–7. *Access to the motif is made by sawing from the edge of the material and entering the outline of the design at a certain point to disguise its entry.*

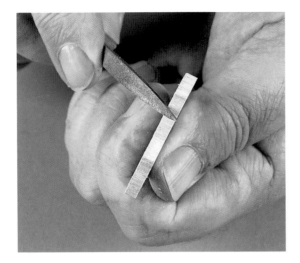

13–8. *The lower edge of the motif is trimmed to avoid any impediment to its entry into the recess.*

13–9. *The router-base attachment shown is dedicated for use with mini-power tools.*

13–10. *A down-cut router bit is fitted into the chuck of the mini-power tool.*

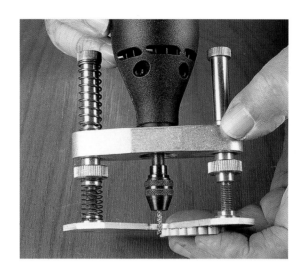

13–11. *All parts are assembled, ready to begin excavation of the recess—but not before the depth of the cutter is adjusted to match the thickness of the motif.*

13–12. *A further check is made to be sure of the cutter depth-setting.*

13–13. *A fine-bladed and well-sharpened knife is used to outline the motif on the ground. It is clamped firmly between the jaws of the vise and rests on the worktop.*

13–14. *A clear view is provided through the base aperture of the cutter at work, showing routing in progress.*

13–15. *Motif and recess are matched and ready for insertion.*

13–16. *After gluing and leveling, the smoothed surface has been given a coat of oil to seal it.*

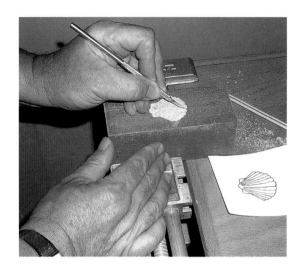

13–17. *The convolutions of the shell used in the design are incised with a knife and emphasized with ink.*

13–18. *A few more rubs with an oiled cloth impart a glow to the finished inlay.*

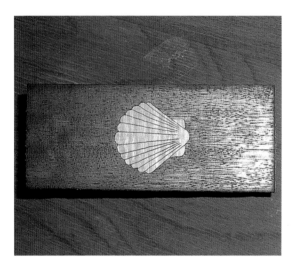

13–19. *The inlayed motif.*

CHAPTER 14

INLAYING A MOTIF-AND-LINE COMBINATION

In this demonstration, a pair of corner motifs and lines are combined in an ensemble, suitable for a box lid or a decorative panel. Hand tools are used throughout to inlay the proprietary motifs and standard lines.

14–2. *Using a fine-pointed drafting pencil, mark the outlines of the corner motifs. Give the two motifs marks to assist in identification later.*

Use either a scalpel blade or needle point or fine-lead drafting pencil to mark the outlines of the motifs. No need to mark out the channels for the lines this time.

Having marked each field with some identification to be sure of inlaying each motif in its own recess, set them aside now.

Using a scalpel or craft knife, trace the pencil marks with the lightest touch, barely inserting the point of the blade. All that is required at this first pass is to emphasize the outline of the motif, and this requires a disciplined concentration.

Caution should be used when marking, and having completed the outlining with the knife, one may continue to increase the depth of the cut a little at a time. A more substantial blade than a scalpel is needed for this operation. Each subse-

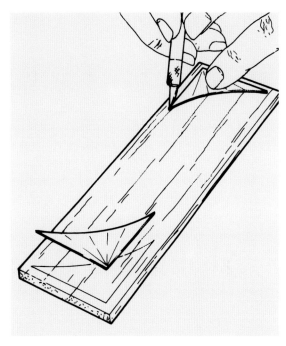

quent pass should be little more than resting the knife firmly, rather than pressing heavily, because the main intention is to follow the line accurately. Only a few seconds are involved in the operation anyway, so no great saving is made by hurrying. Better to take a few more light passes than risk straying from the correct incised path.

OPPOSITE **14–1.** *A pair of corner motifs, as supplied, are mounted in a protective ground, from which they must be trimmed.*

It is necessary to trim the corner motifs from the protective mounts in which they are delivered from the supplier. This should be done with great care, since the outer portions of the design may become detached if handled roughly. The lines that will be applied to join the two corners should be passed through the thicknessing tool (see Chapter 8) to bring them to uniform size. Thicknessing should be done before adjusting the scratch stock blade to the required width. In arranging the elements to be inlaid, consideration must be given to the placing of the lines. Not only will the lines connect the two motifs, but they should also lie parallel to the edge of the ground. The reason for this is to permit the channel cutter to make the line grooves by using its fence as a guide along the edge of the ground.

In order to reduce the leveling process to a minimum, the ground is prepared to size and given a flat and smooth, but not polished, surface.

The best positions are visualized for the inlays, in accordance with their proportions and the shape of the ground. Before marking out the selected elements, they are laid out in the positions they will occupy when inlaid. When a satisfactory arrangement is resolved, mark the outlines of the corner motifs first. Do not assume that they are identical; they may not be, so it's better to work on them individually and make sure to keep them separate.

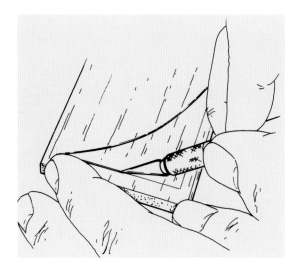

14–3. *A razor-sharp pointed blade is needed for secondary marking and deepening the outline of the recess.*

Judge by the amount of inserted blade as to the depth reached by its point. For instance, the knife shown in this demonstration is triangular. Its insertion is twice the width at any given point, making it an easy job to estimate how deep the point has penetrated. Since most motifs are not much thicker than a hefty postcard, the necessary depth is not difficult to achieve.

14–4. *The recess is excavated with a hand router, with the edge on the router blade made as sharp as possible. Its depth is set at half the thickness of the motif, in preparation for the first cut—during which only half the depth of the motif will be removed.*

It is best to work around the periphery, removing a strip at a time, using short strokes toward the marked or incised outline. Optimum control is applied, pushing down and forward, constantly ready to pull back or stop the forward movement if there is the slightest danger of over-shooting the line.

When a shallow trench has been made all around, the central section may be removed to produce a provisional "floor."

In resetting the router blade for the final depth of the recess, consider that in the final process, when leveling the motif and the ground, it is better to remove superfluous material from the motif than

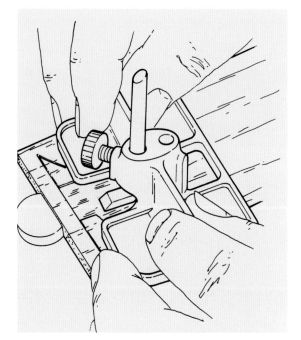

from the surface of the ground. Therefore, assess the depth needed to leave the very slightest amount of the motif protruding above the ground level and set the blade accordingly. For example, measure the thickness of the motif and reduce the amount by about 5 percent, and set the blade to remove waste to that depth.

Care is still required with the second cut, even though the edges of the recess may be well-defined. Slips may still occur in the routing and it is all too easy to remove a piece of the periphery by accident.

If a vernier caliper is available, it would be well-employed for this job, as shown in Chapter 10.

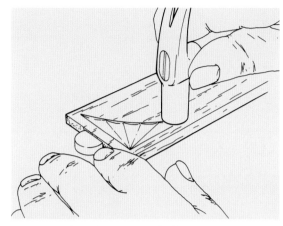

14–6. *In this illustration, the hammer is not striking the motif—the hammerhead is being pressed to localize the pressure, thus embedding the motif.*

Assuming that all is well up to this point in the project, it is best to embed the motifs before continuing with the inlaying of the lines. A hammer was used to apply pressure to embed the motifs, and clamps were used with pads for absolute security. An example of this procedure is shown in the last chapter. It is wise to place a piece of paper between the clamping pad and the motif to avoid the risk of a sticky problem if glue escapes.

The Holtey channel cutter is used to mark the sides of the grooves for the lines. (See Chapter 8.) In fact, as the lines are parallel and straight, the channel incisions could be achieved with a steel ruler and a knife. Following this, the shop-made scratch stock is used to groove out the channels for the lines. The scratch-stock blade is ground to match the width of the lines.

Before incising the channels for the lines, needless to say, a test run with scrap material is made. A cautious pass is then taken along the ground without actually incising, to be sure that the distance from the edge was correctly positioned to connect the marked lines as planned.

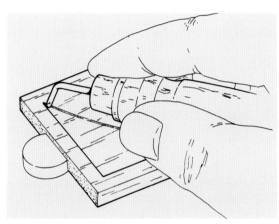

14–5. *The toothpick chisel is used to tease out the waste from corners that are inaccessible to the router blade and to ensure that no crumbs are left to hamper the embedding of the motif.*

One "dry" run, without glue, should suffice to check the fit of the motif in the recess. There should not be any discrepancies, but if there are it may be useful to look over the section on Troubleshooting in Chapter 10.

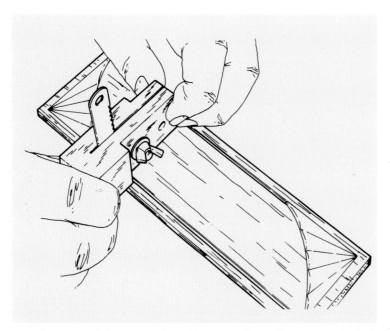

14–7. *The scratch stock is used to excavate the channel for the lines. The desirable practice of lightly scoring with the blades, before the actually incising, should now be a habit. In this particular case, since the grain runs with the length, in a strong fibrous material, all the more discretion is needed to guard against the blade's veering toward a strong grain, causing a deviation from the line. This condition is not dangerous if the grain runs in toward the center of the ground, because the fence bearing against the edge prevents the blade from following. If, however, the grain wanders toward the outer edge, effort must be made to dissuade the blade from potential misdirection.*

Assuming the channel cutting is achieved successfully, it is then necessary to remove the waste. A toothpick chisel could be used, but a more satisfactory effect is achievable with the scratch tool due to its fence acting as a secure guide. It also has the facility to regulate the depth of the recess by setting the blade correctly. Care must be exercised in grinding the blade width to suit the line to be inlaid —and don't forget, first try it on a piece of scrap.

Removal of the waste should not present a problem if extra care is taken at the ends of the channel, where contact is made between the lines and the inlaid motifs. Nothing should be left to chance in this respect, using the toothpick chisel to remove the waste immediately in front of the embedded motifs, before the application of the scratch stock.

When the waste has been excavated to the correct depth, and the toothpick chisel has been employed as needed to remove any superfluity from the channel, it is brushed clean to accept the line.

A small amount of glue is laid into the channel and the lines. It is applied with pressure and retained with masking tape until dry.

Routine cleaning up of the surfaces of all the inlaid elements and the ground should not present any problems if the preceding stages have been carried out correctly. There is always the inherent possibility that a small piece of the inlay may pop out during the leveling. If this does happen, it is most likely to be in the initial passes of the scraper. Therefore, it is during the early part of this operation that scrupulous examination be given to the inlays, hopefully to discover nothing missing. If a portion has become detached (providing that it is recoverable, undamaged, and complete), it should be an easy matter to replace it with a dab of glue. Thorough drying should follow before a return to the scraping operation, hopefully to reveal an attractive inlaid decoration.

14–8. *The motif-and-line inlay combination is completed, with a wipe-over of finishing oil to enhance the grain.*

14–9. *Detail of a panel inlaid in the fingerboard of a Renaissance lute made by the author. The motif was constructed from rosewood with tulipwood stringing. Inlaying this panel was a similar operation to that demonstrated in the motif-and-line project. A fine ebony and pear purfling was added to decorate the pointed "moustaches" where the fingerboard and soundboard meet.*

CHAPTER 15

INLAYING A ROSETTE

A rosette is an ornamentation, usually of foliage or floral design, that is used as a decorative motif. One of its uses is to decorate the sound hole on musical instruments.

This chapter demonstrates inlaying techniques for rosettes for a guitar. It is presumed that the instrument to be inlaid is a classical design in the Spanish style, and not a modern version with a plastic ring masquerading ineffectively as a traditional rosette. This decoration surrounds the sound hole and imparts some additional rigidity and protection to that part of the soundboard. It might be claimed that the contemporary plastic variety is equally effective in acoustic terms, but the appearance of the traditional version is likely to gladden more hearts.

The construction of the rosette need not greatly concern the inlayer, since it is usually bought from a specialist supplier. Rosettes may be simple, sophisticated, or astonishing in their complexity, varying in diameter to suit different instruments **(15–1)**. Generally they are about 1/16 inch (1.5 mm) thick and made on the Tunbridgeware principle.

Some special considerations are necessary with regard to the dimensions of the rosette. Inner and outer diameters may vary slightly due to slight differences in the elements within the design. A high-class product will have less variation than one of modest quality.

In order to establish the diameter of the rosette, it is important to appreciate that a single measurement across the diameter is possibly insufficient, bearing in mind the potential for irregularity already mentioned. Consider first the inner diameter. Several measurements should be taken around the clock, so to speak, from 12 to 6, 2 to 8, 4 to 10, taking the average of these to determine the mean diameter. Measure also the width of the ring, more correctly called its annulus, at several points around the ring to find the average. Multiply this by two and add the result to the mean inner diameter, the sum of which should produce the average outer diameter. Verify this by drawing with a compass the inner and outer diameters on a piece of cardboard, and place the rosette in position with pins inserted around the periphery to hold it in place temporarily to permit a close inspection.

If the measurements were taken accurately, the rosette and the inscribed circles should match. If not, it should be apparent where deficiencies lie, and adjustments may be made accordingly. For sure, while a minimal amount of flexing may be exerted on the rosette to increase or decrease the diameters, it is not possible to change the width of the annulus. That is why it is more accurate to add the width of the rosette to the inner diameter rather than measure the outer diameter separately. A test to help prove this would be to draw around the rosette and then construct circles with a compass to match.

It sounds more complicated than it is in practice and there are likely to be other methods, but the author has had no need to seek them, because the way described above has worked perfectly, many times.

The most reliable and normal technique is by use of the circle cutter as shown in some of the photographs. Whatever the design of the circle-cutting tool, it is almost certainly going to have a point to determine the center of the rosette and act as a pivot during the incising. It

must also have a means of holding a blade securely—incorporating adjustment for depth and radius width. A few special accessories are available for attachment to routers, but my preference is for the type shown in the photographs, combined with the hand router for excavation. The procedure is as follows:

Having determined the sizes of inner and outer diameters of the rosette (**15–2** to **15–6**) and marked its intended position on the soundboard (**15–7**), or other ground, the blade is set in the circle cutter to the radius of the inner circle (**15–8** and **15–9**).

With the intention of embedding 95 percent of the thickness of the rosette into the ground, measure that amount on the cutter blade to judge the depth of the incision (**15–10** and **15–11**). Remember to cut slightly deeper than the floor of the recess to ensure clean corners where the sides meet the floor. The operation of cutting the channel sides is uncomplicated, particularly since the lateral control comes from the center pin, leaving the hands to concentrate primarily on consistent depth of the incision. When the inner circle is marked, the same procedure is applied to the outer diameter (**15–12** to **15–16**).

Use of the hand router is detailed in earlier chapters, but it should be mentioned here that, since the soundboard is made from straight-grained softwood of a close texture, it will cut readily in any direction, but beware of becoming overconfident. An accident is always hovering, ready to strike the unwary. Set the blade of the router at about a quarter of the depth for the finished recess and proceed to work from the center of the recess toward the incisions. As with other examples, if the edges are cleared first, it is easier and safer to remove

Text Continues on Page 185

DETERMINING A ROSETTE'S DIAMETERS AND MARKING ITS POSITION

15–1. *There can be little doubt that one of the features most likely to attract admirers of a high-class guitar is the rosette that decorates the sound hole.*

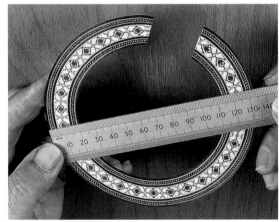

15–2 *to* **15–4.** *Measuring inner and outer diameters across various parts of the rosette.*

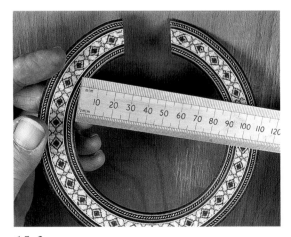

15–3.

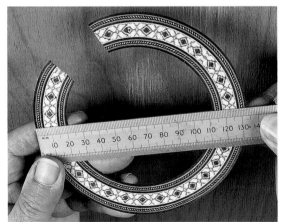

15–4.

DETERMINING A ROSETTE'S DIAMETERS AND MARKING ITS POSITION (continued)

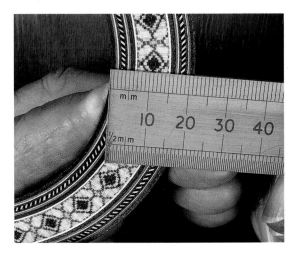

15–5. *Measuring the annulus (the width between the inner and outer diameters) of the rosette ring.*

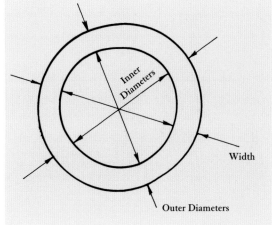

15–6. *Diagram of the dimensions to be taken for calculation of average size of rosette.*

15–7. *A mark is made on the soundboard to locate the intended position of the rosette inlay.*

SETTING THE CIRCLE CUTTER BLADE

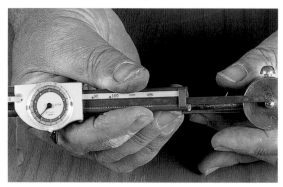

15–8. *Using a steel rule to set a radius on the circle cutter, measuring from the blade edge to the center point. Note: it is easier to locate the center point on a known division on the rule than trying to align the center point with the edge of the rule.*

15–9. *An alternative method of setting the radius of the circle cutter is to use a vernier caliper to measure the distance between the blade edge and the center point.*

MEASURING THE CUTTER BLADE

15–10. *A vernier caliper is used to measure the thickness of the rosette and then used to mark the blade depth in the circle cutter.*

15–11. *A tiny piece of white adhesive tape is applied to the cutter blade to show the depth to which the blade is to be inserted to reach the required depth of the recess. An allowance is made to ensure that a small percentage of the rosette, when inserted, will protrude above the surface of the ground.*

MARKING THE INNER AND OUTER DIAMETERS

15–12. *The inner circle is inscribed first. Only the lightest pressure is applied to mark the circle, reducing the risk of tearing the surface. Several revolutions are made before reaching the depth mark taped on the blade.*

15–13. *Exactly the same technique is made to produce the second, outer-circle incision.*

15–14 *and* **15–15.** *In the photographs only one hand is shown for clarity, but in practice, the circle cutter is best applied with two hands, as shown here. One hand keeps the center point secure and the other hand steers the blade and controls the depth of the incision.*

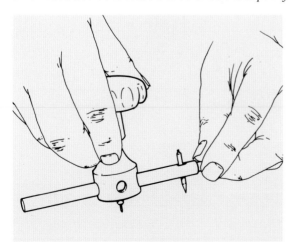

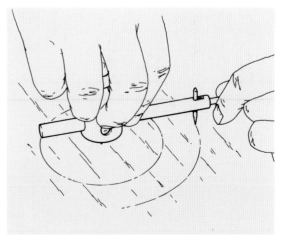

MARKING THE INNER AND OUTER DIAMETERS (continued)

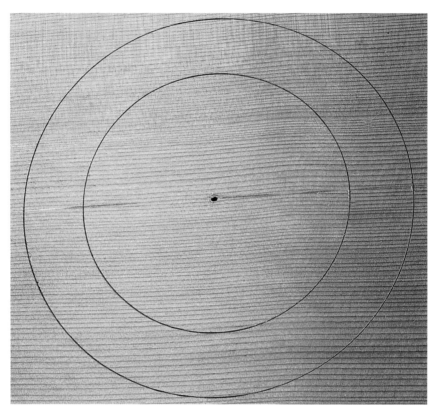

15–16. *Both concentric circles are marked. A third, inner circle will be cut later, to form the sound hole, but not until after the rosette is fitted.*

REMOVING WASTE

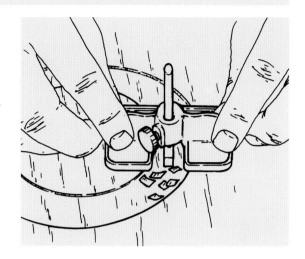

15–17. *Only the lightest possible cut is made for the removal of the first layer of the recess. A cut of 1/64th inch (.5 mm) is sufficient, thus allowing control of the router without impediment.*

15–18. *Three depths of recess are cut with the hand router, each pass removing only the thinnest slices of material. This system reduces risk of accidents and leaves a cleanly excavated floor.*

15–19. *Rosette and recess are aligned and inspected fastidiously before the embedding is performed with adhesive.*

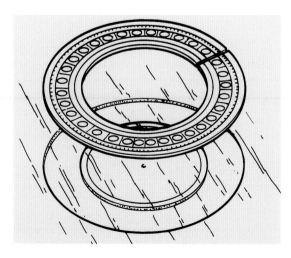

GLUING THE ROSETTE INTO THE RECESS

15–20. *Adhesive is "painted" onto the floor of the recess. Any excess will be squeezed up the sides between the recess and the inlay.*

15–22. *Strong spring clamps are applied to maintain pressure on the rosette during the drying time.*

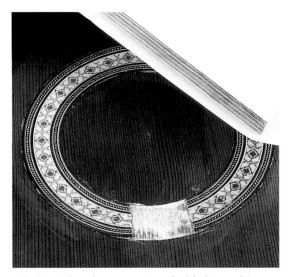

15–21. *After the rosette is embedded into the recess, a waste-paper shield is placed beneath the clamping board. The clamping board is plastic-faced, and therefore resists adhesion with conventional glues.*

15–23. *Leveling is performed with a scraper. Gentle but firm application is recommended with a freshly sharpened blade.*

FINISHING THE ROSETTE

15–24. *A resilient rubbing block is prepared with a fine abrasive sheet.*

15–25. *Several grades of abrasive are used, progressing gradually to very fine, to produce a blemish-free finish.*

15–26. *Finishing oil is applied to the surface with a soft brush.*

FINISHING THE ROSETTE (continued)

15–27. *Wiping over the freshly oiled surface removes surplus oil and prevents pooling. Six or seven coats of oil are brushed on, allowing each to dry out. Then the surface is rubbed down again with the finest abrasive, before applying the next coat.*

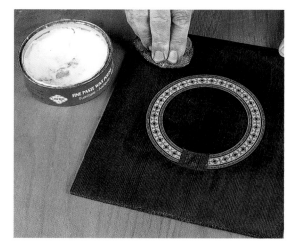

15–28. *A final treatment of wax is applied with a pad of fine wire wool. This not only spreads the wax lightly, it also removes any minor superfluity from the surface.*

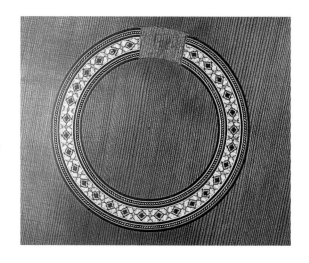

15–29. *The finished inlay glows with the burnished wax finish, fit for a fine guitar. A pity it is embedded into a sample.*

waste from the center of the recess. Repeat this until the full depth is achieved **(15–17 to 15–19)**.

Gluing in of the rosette should present no problem, following a dry run to see that the size of the recess matches. A block and clamp with the usual paper "washer" between is applied to be certain of embedding the rosette to the floor of the recess **(15–20** and **15–21)**.

After thorough drying **(15–22)**, the inlay and ground should be leveled with a carefully applied scraper; frequent visual inspections should be made to detect any detachment of parts of the inlaid element **(15–23)**. As to the surface treatment, this will vary from maker to maker **(15–24** to **15–29)**.

CHAPTER 16

INLAYING PURFLING

Musical instruments, especially the stringed family, have for centuries provided craftsmen with vehicles for decoration, and most often with inlay. Some may suggest that decoration has been made with possible detriment to their acoustic qualities, but that would be difficult to prove, however logical.

In the violin family there is a case for inlay performing the dual function of ornament and support, as in the application of purfling around the edges of the top and bottom plates of the instrument. The inset purfling actually binds the grain, especially the soft spruce soundboard, helping prevent splitting of the vulnerable areas where end grain is exposed. Little or no effect on the acoustic properties would result from this inlay, since it is placed

over the ribs, and rarely encroaches into the area of the instrument's vibrating plates. In any case, by now almost all violins are purfled in this manner and if there were any detectable effect on the sound-producing properties, due to the inlay, it has become an accepted characteristic of the instrument. From the run-of-the-mill fiddles of student quality to the Cremonese masterpieces played by virtuosi, purfling has become a standard feature common to all.

Amazingly, it is the same, disarmingly simple, type of inlay used throughout: a string made up of three pieces side by side, in a black/white/black arrangement. The outer black lines are usually ebony and the nominally "white" is generally sycamore, occasionally the more richly colored pear. The width

Text Continues on Page 194

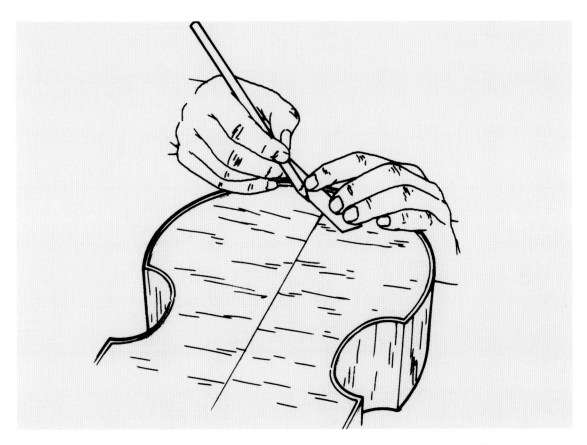

16–1. *Precise marking of the design is essential as the first step. Taking the back of a treble viol as an example: It will be already attached to the ribs (the sides) of the instrument. In constructional terms, the body of the viol will be complete.*

Frequent movements of the workpiece will be necessary, so it is important to cover the worktop with a resilient, nonskid, cloth to prevent damage to the soft soundboard.

Work on the purfling begins with tracing the design with a well-sharpened pencil, or with one of the fine-leaded drafting types with the collet grip. With a rule to measure and assist with incising, it should not present a problem once a satisfactory pattern has been designed. Obviously, a preplanned design should have been made before starting to incise the instrument. Many traditional examples of the latter are in existence for reference, or a new design may be created.

Light marking with the pencil permits some correcting if accidents happen.

When the pencil lines are completed, it is necessary to incise them to the correct depth for the channel. Several ways are possible, but the following is recommended: Incise one of the two lines all around the pattern, observing where the design stops and starts to give the weaving effect. This first incision, as in all cases, should be light, and faithful to the pencil line. It is an opportunity of refining the pencil mark if minor deviations are found in the original marking.

Having defined the line with this incision, it becomes necessary to establish the second line, and this requires some careful consideration. A word about channel width: Hot glue will swell the purfling, so allowance must be made in estimating its fit in the channel. Odd-leg dividers are used for this operation and their setting is crucial to the success of the inlaying. In testing, as always, verify the size on a piece of scrap; try to achieve an easy, slide-in match between the purfling and the channel without pressure.

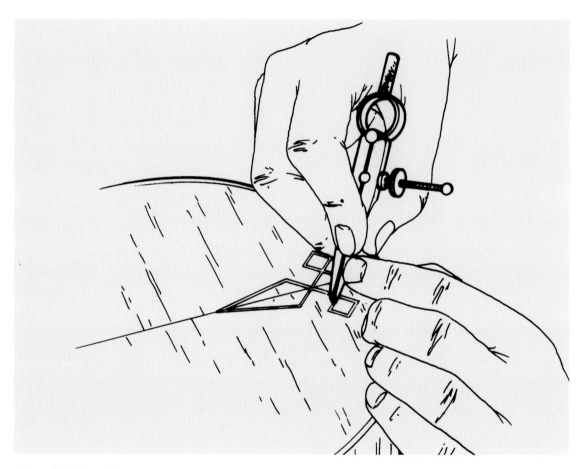

16–2. *"Odd-legs" dividers are shown in action—marking the double recess for the purfling channel.*

Taking the odd-legs dividers, place the longer leg in the incised line, and track along it, cutting the second line with the shorter leg, automatically parallel with the first. Some fastidious care must be taken with stops and starts of lines, especially where they intersect. These areas may need to be refined with the knife.

After completion of this initial definition of the channel, the incision must be deepened to accept 95 percent of the depth of the purfling. Use the knife for this purpose, measuring with the vernier caliper along the blade to assess how much of the point is to be inserted to achieve the correct depth. It is possible to add a strip of adhesive tape to the blade to indicate the required depth of the incision. At this point, it is worth reiterating that this incision should be slightly deeper than the floor of the channel to ensure clean corners where the sides meet the bottom.

In this operation, work the knife from the corners with a slightly downward stabbing action, drawing away along the lines, to be sure of producing clean channels at the ends.

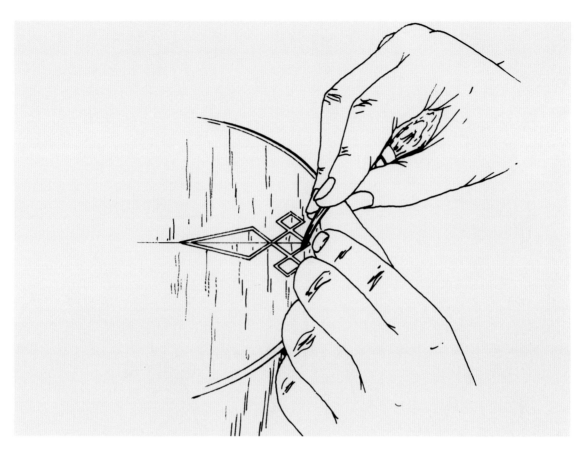

16–3. *Now the channel is excavated by removing the waste. For this, the toothpick chisel is handy. There is a sense of satisfaction as the waste is eased out of the channel and the redundant material pops out. Best to work on short portions at a time, with frequent measurements taken to verify the accuracy of the depth being reached. Use a small piece of the purfling to check or set the depth gauge on the vernier caliper, for testing if it is narrow enough to enter the channel. If the waste is cleared all around and every superfluity removed (inspect with magnifying glasses to be absolutely sure of this), the next stage is the delicate fitting of the purfling.*

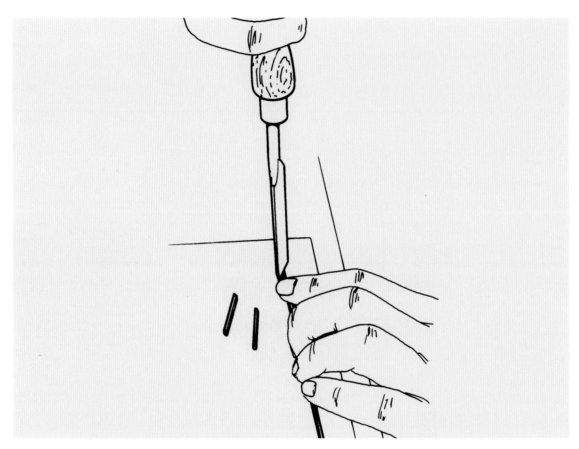

16–4. *Down-stabbing to produce a clean and vertical cut for precise miter joints.*

Accurate preparation of the purfling is of paramount importance. The length of the strips and mitered angles are crucial, imposing the need for some trial and error. Remember, it is not possible to squeeze in an oversize length of purfling without it showing some distortion. Neither is it possible to make up a gap, caused by a deficiency of length, with some type of paste filler—a disguise that will not only be easily detected, but it may even emphasize the fault.

Cutting the purfling to length is best carried out with a chisel used in a downward shearing action. This makes it easier to produce not only a vertical face but also a straight-line cut for a precise miter joint.

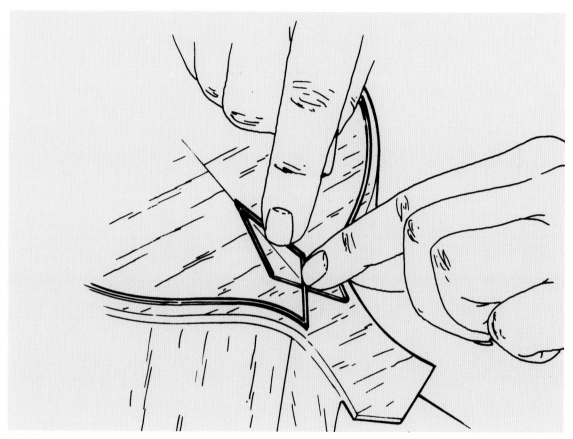

16–5. *Marriage of the parts during the fitting calls for patience, discipline, and aesthetic discernment.*
Fitting adjacent elements means confirming their mitered relationship. Symmetry and equality is possible only if identical joints are produced. Every effort must be concentrated on the achievement of this aim. If this means scrapping some parts, so be it. Purfling is not expensive, so be sure to overstock in case of accidents. It is best to complete a dry run with all elements fitted before any gluing.

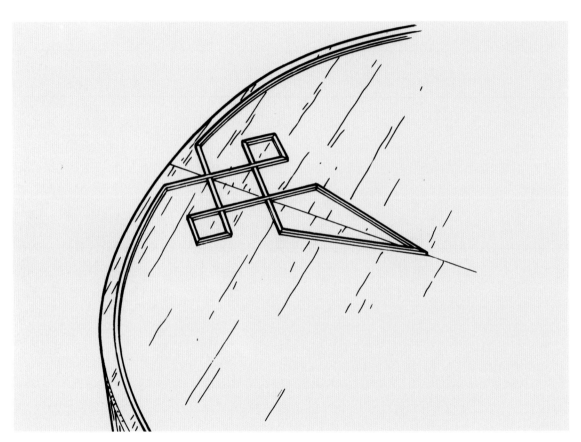

16–6. *All of the elements are fitted and glued, ready for leveling.*

It is best to use a traditional hot glue, for the simple reason that it is possible to be reversed in case of the need to reposition or remove the purfling for any reason. It will probably be unnecessary to clamp the inlay or subject it to more than gentle pressure to embed it. Hot glue may be reactivated by applying heat to a glued joint, permitting separation of the parts for repair or renewel. Heat may be applied by resting a hot knife on the joint.

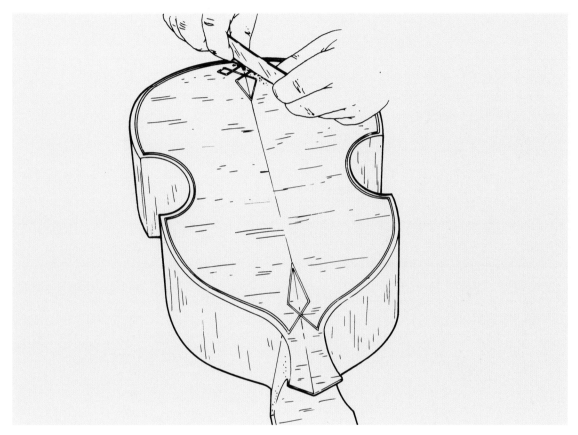

16–7. *A freshly sharpened scraper should be used to scrape the surface of the purfling smooth and level the ground. The questions are: Clean the purfling? Smooth the purfling?*

varies to suit the differing sizes of the instrument's family from violin to contrabass, to satisfy the observation of proportional aesthetics demanded by both craftsman and player. Despite the apparent similarity suggested by a casual glance, close examination of a fine instrument, master-crafted by an expert, will reveal subtle characteristics in the refinement of the application, sometimes enough to identify the individual luthier.

In the viol family, the early cousins of the violin, purfling is not always restricted to the edge of the instrument, but it may also be applied to the other flat areas such as the back. Geometric forms are extended from the edge purfling in designs with their origins in Celtic and Moorish knot patterns. Here the luthier must have some expertise to decide which elements in the design are to "cross over" others. At points where the lines appear to cross, one over the other, the object is to emphasize the illusion by cutting the inlays to give an over-and-under effect as in weaving.

Illus. **16-1** to **16-8** show how it is done.

16–8. *Double purfling on a viol back made by the great British luthier, Jane Julier. Her instruments are not only the most highly respected for their magnificent craftsmanship, they are the choice of the world's virtuosi for their outstanding tonal qualities.*

CHAPTER 17

CREATING AN INLAY FOR AN EXISTING RECESS

If an inlay is to be replaced into an existing recess, as in the case of a repair, it is a straightforward process. This process is detailed in **17–1** to **17–4**. As shown in the illustrations, thin paper is placed over the recess and a soft crayon is used to trace the outline of the recess onto the paper. The paper, of course, is glued to the motif material. The author's preference is to use an old-fashioned fretsaw to cut out the motif—especially when cutting out small, individual items.

FITTING THE MOTIF

Now make a trial fit of the motif and recess **(17–5)**. If they fit, glue the motif in place **(17–6)**. Assuming the motif has been cut out, the paper pattern may be removed. If it does not come off easily, it doesn't matter, because the leveling process will remove it **(17–7 and 17–8)**. At least, any adhering paper will identify the top from the bottom, ensuring its insertion the right way up.

REPLACING AN INLAY

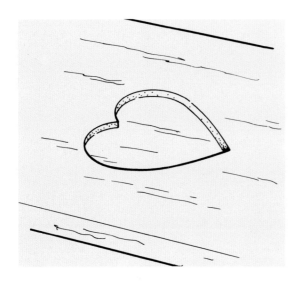

17–1. *An existing recess that has lost its inlay.*

The procedure to create and fit a suitable motif is as follows: Inspect the surface immediately surrounding the recess. If dents or defects have occurred to spoil the possibility of producing a clean edge joint between the recess and the motif, it may be necessary to recut the sides. A sharp knife, a keen eye, and a steady hand are the order of the day.

Assuming that either the edge was acceptable or that it has been corrected, choose a piece of suitable material for the motif. If other inlaid elements are present then these must be referred to, to help decide. Usually an inlay is made with a material that contrasts in color to the ground.

Measure the depth of the recess with a vernier caliper and bring the inlay material to suitable thickness. Best to make it slightly thicker than the recess depth to create a slight protrusion after fitting. It is then easy to clean back the motif level with the ground, rather than the other way around.

17–2. *A soft crayon is used to trace on paper the outline of the recess.*

Take a piece of thin paper and place it over the recess. Using a soft, waxy crayon, rub across the paper over the recess. This should define the shape of the recess, even to the detail of scars and blemishes.

Secure the paper pattern to the surface of the inlay material with adhesive and allow it to set.

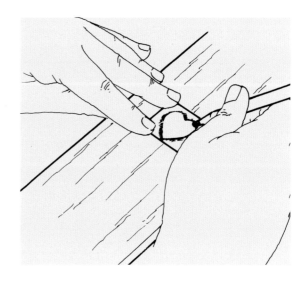

REPLACING AN INLAY (continued)

17–3. *After the preparation of the tracing, the paper is glued to the material chosen for the motif.*

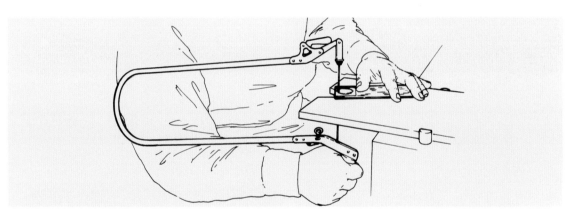

17–4. *An old-fashioned Hobbies fretsaw is used for cutting out the motif. Notice the technique of resting the frame of the saw along the arm. Raising and lowering the saw by pivoting at the elbow creates a machine-like movement.*

Cutting with a hand fretsaw is the author's preference, particularly if making a small, individual item. The hand fretsaw is still used for the very finest of inlaid marquetry work and has every right to be considered alongside its younger relative, the powered scroll saw.

If the saw-frame is held in contact with the arm, and the elbow acts as a pivot, a vertical reciprocation may result, similar to that effected by machine scroll saws. Or is it the other way around?

To give support to the workpiece during the sawing operation, an auxiliary table with a V-notch cut in the front, for saw-blade access, is attached to the bench top.

The machine scroll saw performs the same task as the hand-held fretsaw, but it oscillates much faster than the human arm and also with a controlled vertical movement. This is suitable for cutting wood up to 2 inches (50 mm) thick. A professional-quality, heavy-duty model will cut from the thinnest veneers up to 4 inches (100 mm) thick.

Assuming that the sawing process is completed, whether by hand or machine, the motif is placed gently over the recess. Any dissimilar features should be noticeable. If the motif is oversized in any area, corrections can be made by filing or rubbing down with an abrasive paper. However, if the problem is an undersized motif, another should be made, hopefully, to produce a closer fit.

FITTING THE MOTIF

17–5. *Motif and recess are a good match and ready for fitting.*

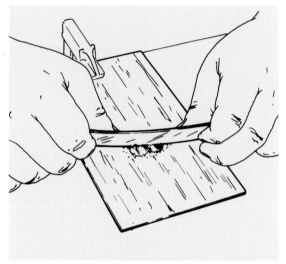

17–7. *Superfluous material is scraped off to level the surfaces. This is followed by polishing to suit the original finish.*

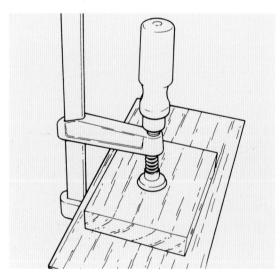

17–6. *Pressure is applied with a clamp and pad during the gluing process. A little scrape around the bottom corner of the motif removes any ragged edges that might hinder its placing, and a trial fit is made, but without fully inserting the motif into the recess. If all is well, then it may be glued into position and clamped until dry.*

17–8. *With both the motif and ground leveled, a clean face is ready for surface polish. A piece of pine is inlaid with a rosewood heart to represent the repaired subject.*

CHAPTER 18

INLAY GALLERY

The photos in this chapter demonstrate the range of artistic expression and practical considerations possible with inlaying.

18–1. *A simple tablet of common softwood may be enhanced with a clean black corner banding.*

18–2. *Giovanni Aversa is a marquetry artist who creates his own designs and applies them to articles such as this trinket box.*

18–3. *An incised and carved rose adorns the soundboard on this lute, designed and built by the author. Rosewood and tulipwood are used in the inlaid panel in the fingerboard.*

18–4. *This is Tunbridge ware, a traditional craft recently revitalized by William Adams. It is a form of mosaic assembled in long strips and sliced into thin tiles, all showing identical features.*

18–5. *Tunbridge ware is applied to turned objects, with inlays made by William Adams.*

18–6. *Double-purfling decorates the border of this viol soundboard by Jane Julier, an outstanding luthier with an international reputation for her superb instruments.*

18–7. *Knot patterns with the illusion of woven lines are the feature of the purfling inlaid in the back of this Jane Julier viol.*

18–8. *Inlaid purfling adorns the edges and the center joint in the back of this guitar, made by the author. It is built on traditional classical Spanish lines.*

18–9. *Inlays are also featured in the front of the guitar, and around the edges, the bridge, and the rosette decorating the sound hole.*

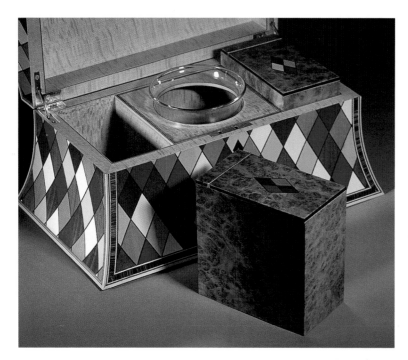

18–10. *Andrew Crawford's work is highly acclaimed, not only for its fine craftsmanship, but also for his artistic treatment of materials combining appearance with function.*

18–11. *A classical guitar in Brazilian rosewood and cedar with various inlays.*

18–12. *The rosette decorating the sound hole is made by the traditional Tunbridge method. Composite elements make up the corner banding. (See Chapter 9 for information on corner banding.)*

18–13. *A renaissance lute. The body is made of bird's-eye maple, and the soundboard of spruce. The sound hole is decorated in fine fretwork.*

APPENDIX A: TREATING THE FINISHED SURFACE

Surface treatment is one of those subjects that could be given endless attention and fill volumes, and it has. Students may enjoy some further research on the subject to get the best out of their materials and projects. For now, try the following quick, easy, and sure way to a respectable, foolproof finish!

It is assumed that a smooth and level surface has been prepared, without scratches or scuffs. Holding the work up to a directional light source such as a conventional tungsten lightbulb or the sun, reflections should show clearly any discrepancies. Any shortcomings will be emphasized and should be corrected.

Any one of the following respected brands of Danish, teak, finishing, or similar oils may be applied to the raw surface. Plain or boiled linseed oil will do, in a pinch, but the ones mentioned by name are easily and quickly applied without any special knowledge. Some slight variations in application may pertain, as may be indicated by scrutiny of the instructions that come with the individual brands.

With a soft cloth or brush, give a generous application of oil to the surface, working well into the grain and removing, before it dries, any surplus pools by wiping over with a soft dry cloth. Let it dry and admire the immediate effect of the oil.

Rub down the dried, oiled surface, using either very fine abrasive papers or the finest wire wool. Apply several more coats of the oil, drying and rubbing down in between coats. When the whole surface has a buildup of dry oil, take a proprietary wax polish, preferably beeswax-based, available in semi-solid quality in cans. Use a clean cloth, or even an unused piece of wire wool, and rub over the surface lightly with the wax polish. Buff it up immediately with another clean cloth to make a soft sheen. More wax and more burnishing may be applied to give a deeper gloss, if required.

Now you can stand back and reflect on, and in, your beautiful work.

Applying a coat of wax polish to the surface of a marquetry project with a pad of wire wool, to produce a silky finish of great depth and quality.

APPENDIX B: SAFETY

It is all too easy to leave considerations of safety until last, or even to ignore it altogether, because accidents won't happen, will they? And anyway it's a boring topic, isn't it? Maybe, but safety awareness is essential to complete the workshop environment.

Few items of equipment found in the average home-based workshop are likely to turn on their owners without provocation, but hazards may be encountered, especially if the owner is indifferent to basic safety procedures.

On the principle that prevention is better than an insurance claim, the following is intended to help avoid common accidents. The list is not presented in order of priority:

SECURITY AND FIRE PRECAUTIONS

Keep the workshop door locked when unoc-cupied, to prevent the entry of unaccompanied children or the inexperienced.

Ask the local fire-prevention officer for any advice on this subject, especially if there are unusual features pertaining to your situation. Consider the highly flammable nature of adhesives, polish, varnish, and spirits of various kinds, all of which may be needed from time to time. Add to this the stock of woods, paper, cleaning cloths, and other associated items and we have the ingredients for a firebomb that would gladden the heart of any arsonist. Flammable liquids should be kept securely stored away from accidental contact, preferably in a fireproof cabinet (B-1). If the cabinet is wood, then the flammable items should be stored in a metal container within it.

Cloths, tissues, and steel wool used for cleaning surfaces or mopping up spilled glues

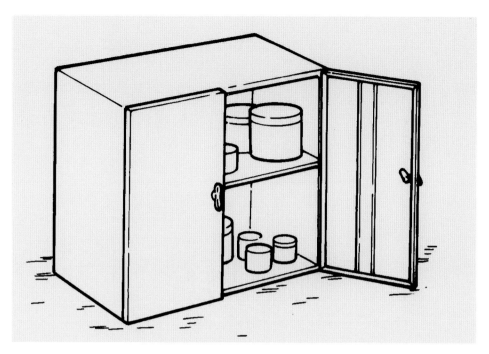

B–1. *A steel cabinet for the safe storage of flammable items.*

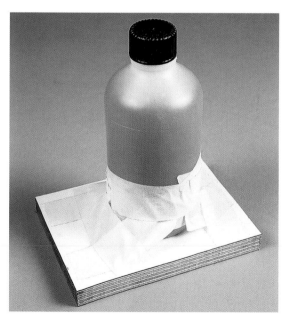

B–2. *When applying varnish, oils, or other surface finishes with a potential for disaster, it makes sense to avoid accidental spillage by taping the container to a base, to bolster its stability.*

and polishes should be either cleaned or destroyed after use. A wad of steel wool charged with waste rubbings from varnished work is a dormant explosive predisposed to spontaneous combustion if conditions are favorable. And remember that some finishes are potentially hazardous **(B–2)**.

On the occasions when heat is being used, as in the case of heating sand, etc., or in any situation where naked flame is present, there is always a potential for disaster. Sensible precautions must be taken to comply with recommended safety regulations applicable to the heat source.

Check that appropriate firefighting apparatuses of the correct type for any eventuality are present.

Lighting
Whether relying on a natural light source or

B–3. *Facial protection with a dust mask and safety glasses.*

B–4. *Overalls with real pockets and tight cuffs.*

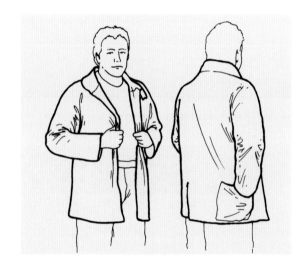

B–5. *This pair of strong boots will protect feet from falling tools; it also has nonskid soles, to prevent slippage.*

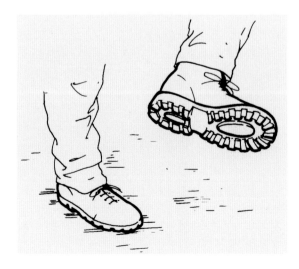

artificial illumination, lighting of the work area is crucial to the success of the work process and to personal safety. Correct siting of light sources applies also to the illumination of pedestrian areas, which should be clear of obstruction, debris, or any other object that might cause tripping.

ELECTRICITY

1. Double-check wiring, connections, plugs, and sockets in the electrical power supply, verifying that they comply with prevailing regulations and are compatible with the specifications of powered equipment.

2. Make a habit of inspecting power cables for wear or damage and replace them if necessary.

3. Use plugs molded from unbreakable material.

4. During maintenance programs or when undertaking repairs, and in any other situation that requires hands-on contact, with the exception of actually operating power tools, disconnect appliances from the main power supply.

5. Make sure that equipment switches are turned to "off" before activating the power supply.

6. Beware of any insidious dampness, such as might be caused by condensation, encroaching on the electrical circuitry.

WORKSHOP EQUIPMENT AND TOOLS

1. Keep the workplace tidy and free from debris, particularly around the feet.

2. Read workshop manuals, handbooks, and any documents containing advice about the correct use of tools and equipment. Become familiar with any operational controls and switch gear.

3. See that the workbench is strong enough for the work intended and sited securely to remain stable without rocking. Use wedges to fill gaps beneath table legs.

4. Put aside the tools that are not required and only have within arm's reach the items that are needed for the current process.

PERSONAL SAFETY

1. To protect the eyes from flying shards when any machinery is used, wear safety glasses, or, if spectacles are worn, wear protective goggles over them.

2. Any kind of dust is potentially harmful and it doesn't go away when the sawing or the abrading stops. A fabric dust mask helps prevent inhalation of fine dust particles **(B–3)**. If the power tool you are using has a built-in or attachable vacuum facility, use it.

3. Wear clothing that does not have loose, flapping pockets or wide sleeves **(B–4)**.

4. Wear strong shoes to protect from possible damage caused from dropping sharp tools. Best if they have nonslip soles **(B–5)**.

Appendix C: Glossary

Banding (also known as binding) A plain single or multiple strip, for inlaying, usually into a corner rabbet.

Burnisher (also known as "ticketer") A tool made in the likeness of a small butcher's steel, for sharpening knives, but in this case used for turning over the edges of scraper blades to create a burr.

Circle Cutter Used for marking or cutting circular lines. A blade is fitted into a cross-shaft, adjustable to and from a central point used as a pivot; it is similar in principle to a pair of compasses.

Ditching Used to describe the delineation of the periphery of a "field," or recess, by channeling in preparation for the clearing of the inner waste from its floor.

Fence A guide, or bearing, against which a workpiece or other material may rest for repetitive actions, or to produce a parallel reference for cutting or other operations.

Fishtail Chisel So-called because of its appearance, being wider at its cutting edge than in the shank.

Fretsaw Traditional name for what is now more commonly called a scroll saw. There is the tendency to call the manual variety a fretsaw, and the machine type scroll saw.

Ground The item or material into which an inlay is to be embedded.

Hand Router A tool whose main feature is a cranked cutter, adjustable for depth of cut, which is used to rout out waste.

Kerf A slot, or gap, left in the workpiece by sawing.

Line Band, binding, or stringing that is usually square in section, plain, a solid, single-color material, and comparatively small.

Lutherie From the old term meaning literally "lute-making," and now taken to mean the making of any type of musical instrument.

Marquetry The cutting and gluing side by side of decorative wood pieces, usually from veneers. Natural characteristics of the grain, texture, and color are employed to create a pictorial effect.

MDF The recognized abbreviation for medium-density fiberboard, a material developed in the United States by binding together resin wood fibers by rolling and pressing and cutting sheets to size.

Miter Guide A tool, fixed at useful angles, such as 30, 45 or 60 degrees, that is used similarly to a set square to establish the angles of miter joints.

Motif A distinctive idea or theme elaborated into a shape or pattern as a design for, in this instance, inlaying.

Odd-Leg Dividers Dividers made from a pair of divider calipers that have legs of unequal lengths. The end of each leg is ground to a knife point to permit marking or incising. The point of the longer leg is inserted into an existing incision, which is used as a guide. As it is traversing, the point of the shorter leg marks or incises a line parallel to the original.

Purfling The type of string or band inlay associated with musical instruments. It consists of a central strip contrasting in color to the two outer strips.

Purfling cutter More correctly named channel cutter, a tool used for marking or incising channels to receive purfling and not, as its name suggests, to cut purfling.

Rabbet (also known as rebate) A recess along the edge of a ground or workpiece to form a channel to receive an inlaid part.

Rosette A circular arrangement of wooden ribbons or strips enclosing a Tunbridge ware

pattern of geometrical forms.

Router A portable power tool with a built-in electric motor to drive cutters of the rotary type, used for plunge boring or side cutting to produce channels. It may be used freehand, with accessories, or attached to a table.

Scratch Stock A tool used to cut grooves or to work moldings. Made in the workshop to individual requirements, it consists of two pieces of wood shaped like an inverted "L," clamped with screws to hold the cutter. It works on the principle of a scraper and may be used to cut "stopped" grooves and to follow curved edges.

Scroll Saw A motorized saw with a reciprocating vertical movement carrying a fine blade for the cutting of motifs, apertures, and other delicate items.

Seam Roller A roller made from wood or plastic, with a metal spindle held between the forks of a handle, used to roll out joins in paper or any other situation where point pressure is required, uniformly, over a large area.

Stringing (also referred to as string) An inlay of either plain or decorative wood, sometimes called banding, made of either one single piece or multiple strips.

Thicknesser, Stringing A special tool comprising a blade, its holder, and a table. The blade position over the table is adjustable for height, permitting the setting of a gap through which banding or other slender materials may be passed to regulate the uniformity of their thickness. It works on a scraping principle.

Ticketer (see Burnisher)

Toothpick Chisel So-called because of its small size. A cranked blade of steel, inserted into a wooden handle; usually made by the user from a nail.

Tunbridgeware A form of miniature

marquetry associated with the town of Tunbridge Wells, in Kent, England. Square-sectioned strips, of carefully chosen colors, are glued together to form patterns and sliced across into thin tiles. When laid side by side, these tiles may be formed into further designs. The finest are designs that form entire pictorial motifs.

Veneer A thin slice of wood, chosen for its fine appearance and intended to be glued to a material of inferior quality. Cut on special machinery, either by saw, or knife, to thicknesses as little as $\frac{1}{64}$ inch (.6 mm).

Vernier Caliper A precision measuring device incorporating the facility to measure three dimensions: internal, external, and depth.

METRIC EQUIVALENCY CHART

INCHES TO MILLIMETERS AND CENTIMETERS
MM=Millimeters CM=Centimeters

Inches	MM	CM	Inches	CM	Inches	CM
$1/8$	3	0.3	9	22.9	30	76.2
$1/4$	6	0.6	10	25.4	31	78.7
$3/8$	10	1.0	11	27.9	32	81.3
$1/2$	13	1.3	12	30.5	33	83.8
$5/8$	16	1.6	13	33.0	34	86.4
$3/4$	19	1.9	14	35.6	35	88.9
$7/8$	22	2.2	15	38.1	36	91.4
1	25	2.5	16	40.6	37	94.0
$1 1/4$	32	3.2	17	43.2	38	96.5
$1 1/2$	38	3.8	18	45.7	39	99.1
$1 3/4$	44	4.4	19	48.3	48	101.6
2	51	5.1	20	50.8	41	104.1
$2 1/2$	64	6.4	21	53.3	42	106.7
3	76	7.6	22	55.9	43	109.2
$3 1/2$	89	8.9	23	58.4	44	111.8
4	102	10.2	24	61.0	45	114.3
$4 1/2$	114	11.4	25	63.5	46	116.8
5	127	12.7	26	66.0	47	119.4
6	152	15.2	27	68.6	48	121.9

INDEX